North East by Rail

A guide to the routes, scenery and towns

Jarrold Publishing, Norwich

ABOUT THIS BOOK

Welcome to the second, enlarged edition of *North East by Rail*, first published in 1986 by the Railway Development Society – the independent, national voluntary body for rail users – and now part of a series of guide-books covering the whole of Great Britain.

We hope that it will show you, the reader, a pleasant and interesting way of exploring the four counties of North East England, which have some of the oldest railways in the world, and some of the most modern.

As Editor, I am indebted to those local members of the Society who have written so knowledgeably about their local lines and who have made numerous suggestions. Apart from the authors of individual chapters, valuable help has also come from Ruth Clayfield and Messrs E. Maxwell (of the Tanfield Railway Society), A. Walker, G.A. Lillie, T.C. Eden, P. Blackburn and S. Norton.

For the map, our thanks go to Peter Wakefield, while John Brodribb and Bernard Eyre were responsible for the line diagrams. Thanks are also due to the photographers who have allowed us to use their work, and to our publisher for helping us to reach a wide public.

We have made every effort to include up-to-date information. However, as train and especially bus timetables, fares, entrance times and charges can change at quite short notice, we advise you to check these locally and to this end we have given some addresses and telephone numbers.

We have written with the general reader in mind, but the inclusion of some railway history and terminology was inevitable, and will indeed help you to get the most out of your journeys, for railways have played a central role in the development of this region.

The 'up' line or platform is that used by trains to London or another large city; the 'down' line or platform being the opposite. A DMU is a diesel multiple unit train or railcar. 'Pacer' is the name given to a lightweight type of DMU introduced in the late 1980s for local trips, while 'Sprinters' are a group of more powerful DMU types used on longer-distance journeys. An HST (High Speed Train), also known as an InterCity 125, is a fixed-formation express train with a diesel power-car at either end. It can travel at up to 125 mph and is used on many non-electrified main lines.

Britain's railways were built and run by private companies in the nineteenth century. Nearly all of the lines covered by this book were part of the North Eastern Railway, which merged with other companies in 1923 to form the London & North Eastern Railway. In 1948, the companies were nationalised as British Railways, now British Rail.

The BR Chairman in the early 1960s was Dr Richard Beeching, who is chiefly remembered for the large number of closures which took place during and just after his period of office.

Since the early 1970s, there have been very few rail passenger closures, while a considerable number of stations, and some lines, have been reopened. As readers will discover, the North East has its share of such reopenings.

Trevor Garrod
March 1990

Front cover: The train provides a grandstand view of Durham city

Back cover: St Mary's Island, Whitley Bay (*Photo:* Edmund Atkinson)

Title page: Metro train – the fastest way from the centre of Newcastle to the coast (*Photo:* Harold Atkinson)

CONTENTS

KEY TO LINE DIAGRAMS

THIRSK Station name.
Staffed station; rail tickets and information available. Connecting rail service from the station shown.
Unstaffed station; pay guard on train. Through rail service to destination(s) shown on line.

Seaham Station name.

B   Buffet.

D   Disabled 'core' station. Fully accessible to ambulance and wheelchair-bound people. Facilities for hearing- and sight-impaired people.

T   Taxis available.

TC   Travel Centre.

M   Interchange with Tyne & Wear Metro.

KX   London (Kings Cross).

Preserved station, staffed or unstaffed. Services not available at all times.

Closed station.

Principal stations on new Sprinter service.

INTRODUCTION

North East England was the birthplace of the passenger railway, and a visit to this part of the country, more than one and a half centuries later, remains a memorable experience.

The world's first proper passenger railway operated by steam locomotives was the Stockton & Darlington, opened in 1825. Today, that line is part of some 300 miles of route which will carry you from the lush Vale of York to the dunes, rocks and castles of the rugged Northumberland coast; from the heather of the breezy Pennines to the seagulls screaming and swooping over Whitby harbour.

A seat in an InterCity train affords you a grandstand view of the massive Durham cathedral and castle, surrounded on three sides by the winding River Wear.

A ride on Newcastle's ultra-modern Metro, well-integrated with other trains and buses, shows visitors from other cities how efficient and attractive urban rail transport can be.

Diesel railcars give panoramic views of the wooded valleys of rivers like the Tyne and Esk. To complete the varied picture, there are vintage steam trains on the North York Moors Railway (one of the longest preserved lines in Britain) and at sites within easy reach of Newcastle.

Trains can take you to resorts like Whitby, Redcar and Whitley Bay, to historic Hexham and Berwick, and to the threshold of up-to-date shopping centres in Newcastle, Gateshead and Middlesbrough. There is excellent walking country in the Pennine Dales and over the North Yorkshire Moors. Seventy-nine British Rail and forty-four Tyne and Wear Metro stations stand ready for you while short bus or cycle trips from railheads will take you to the unique open-air museum at Beamish; Hadrian's Wall with its Roman sites; the imposing ruins of Guisborough Priory; the ancient Abbey on Lindisfarne; and the beautiful castle and park at Alnwick.

North East England possesses a multitude of historical monuments associated with early English Christendom, the turbulent Middle Ages or the Industrial Revolution. Jarrow, on Tyneside, for example, has ninth-century links with the Venerable Bede and twentieth-century associations with the Hunger Marchers.

Famous men and women from this region include railway pioneers George and Robert Stephenson and Timothy Hackworth, the explorer Captain Cook, and the novelist Catherine Cookson. You can visit places connected with all of them.

Fast modern trains bring this area within easy reach of most parts of England, Wales and Scotland, with recent improvements including new through services to Tyneside from Glasgow and Galloway. This guide will help you to get the most out of your voyage of discovery.

YORK–NEWCASTLE–EDINBURGH
by Trevor Garrod

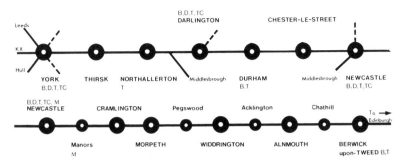

The historic city of York provides a major gateway to the North East. Situated 188½ miles from London's Kings Cross, its majestic station is served by InterCity trains, the fastest of which reach York in just under two hours and then head north to Darlington, Newcastle and Edinburgh. They share the main line north of the city with InterCity 125 trains from the South West and South Wales, via Birmingham and Sheffield, up to Newcastle. Express Sprinter trains from Liverpool, Manchester and Leeds also join the main line here and head up to the North East, and a variety of local services run to York from such places as Hull, Scarborough, Harrogate and West Yorkshire.

As we travel northwards over some twenty miles of straight quadruple track, it is clear that we are on a trunk route, built for speed. Three private companies, the Great Northern, North Eastern and North British Railways, developed it in the nineteenth century as one of the two major railways from England to Scotland. The present-day British Rail refers to this as the East Coast Main Line.

The route was opened in stages between 1841 and 1850. As the companies owning it competed with their rivals on the West Coast Main Line, which ran from London to Glasgow via Crewe and Carlisle, record speeds were set. By 1888, the Kings Cross–Edinburgh run was accomplished in 6 hours 48 minutes; by the late 1920s, powerful Gresley Pacific steam locomotives were running non-stop to Edinburgh in 6 hours.

Diesels started to replace steam in the late 1950s, to be succeeded in turn by the present High Speed Trains or InterCity 125s in the late 1970s. These cut the fastest London–Edinburgh time to 4 hours 35 minutes for a 393-mile journey. The line is now being electrified and a new class of locomotive, the 'Electra', is due to haul the electric trains from 1991 onwards.

The Vale of York is farming country with no large towns, and all but two of the intermediate stations between York and Darlington had closed by 1960. The top expresses speed through the remaining stations, Thirsk and Northallerton, but semi-fast trains call there, giving these two market towns and their wide catchment area a very respectable service.

As we speed across the Vale, note the sign near Tollerton, indicating that we are now half-way between London and Edinburgh, and, to the east of the line, the unusual 'Sidings' restaurant, made up of old restored railway coaches. Further to the north-east, the Howardian Hills and North Yorkshire Moors are looming up, and we can see a white horse, cut into one of the steep hillsides in 1857.

Just over 22 miles from York is Thirsk station, with its two island platforms improved in the 1980s by a district council grant. It is situated about a mile from the town centre, past the well-known racecourse. The town has a population of 6,000,

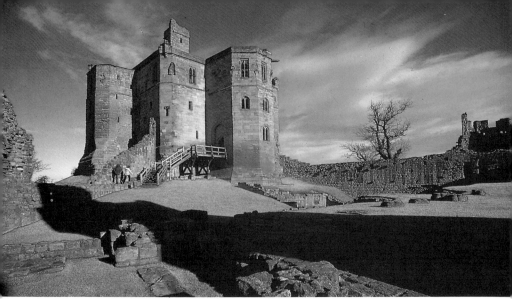

Warkworth Castle

with a Gothic parish church and a museum. There are many miles of flat cycling country and quiet roads around Thirsk, and the North Yorkshire Moors are now close at hand. A pleasant day can be spent cycling eastwards through the Gilling gap in the hills to Malton; or, for those who like long bus rides, travelling along the southern edge of the Moors to Pickering and Scarborough by bus.

On the straight flat track north of Thirsk, a world speed record for diesel trains of 143.2 mph was attained by one of the first InterCity 125s in June 1973.

Seven and three-quarter miles further on, Northallerton can also be used as the railhead for attractive rural rides. This town of 9,000 people grew up as a market and staging-post on the main road, later becoming important for its railway workshops (now closed). Northallerton is also the administrative centre of North Yorkshire, and County Hall can be seen among the trees just to the east of the station.

The main line, quadruple since leaving York, is now double-track, and an avoiding line allows freight trains bound for Teesside to pass to the west of Northallerton station, before rumbling under the main line and off towards Eaglescliffe. The station itself, on an embankment, is denuded of some of its earlier buildings, although some local authority-financed improvements have now been made. It gives good views across the town, dominated by its ornate fourteenth-century church tower.

As your train gathers speed for the next stage north, you may spot a single track trailing in from the west: the freight line up Wensleydale to Leyburn and Redmire. This was used for eight excursion trains between 1978 and 1981 and has been used by several special passenger trains since 1984, but its main traffic is limestone for British Steel from the quarry at Redmire. There are currently three or four buses a day from Northallerton to Leyburn, some of which connect with trains, and from Leyburn you can catch buses to go further up the dale.

Soon the moors are receding to the east, but then the distant Pennines start to take shape to the north-west. Before long we cross a winding river in a deep tree-lined gorge – the Tees, which here forms the boundary between Yorkshire and County Durham. The village of Croft can be seen among trees to the right, and presently we are pulling into Darlington. Nearly all trains call at this imposing station which, together with the town, is described on pages 55–57.

The route north of Darlington passes some derelict sites before reaching open country again, with the pleasant village of Aycliffe to the west, then curving down through undulating farmland with the Great North Road visible on the left. On the opposite side, a double-track line trails in, with a large sign alongside it pointing to Stockton. One wonders for whom this sign is intended, since BR drivers do not normally lose their way. The line forms part of the most direct link from Stockton and the rest of industrial Teesside to Durham and Newcastle, but is only used by passenger trains when there is engineering work in the Darlington area. Then trains are diverted over it and rejoin the main line at Northallerton. RDS and other local campaigners are pressing for a regular passenger service over this route.

Ferryhill village, to the west, lost its station in 1967. Its only connection now with the railway is its junction and the rail-served quarry to the east. At Tursdale Junction, a sign painted on the side of the British Coal workshops informs us that we are 254 miles from London and 8 miles from Durham. Further up the line, graffiti daubed on an overbridge announce, 'This is North East England – R.I.P.'.

The track curves westwards and then northwards again, over the wooded valley of the River Wear with glorious views to the east. Soon we are travelling past an industrial estate and then terraced houses climbing steep slopes before we run into the station at Durham. This handsome edifice was designed as a suitable entrance to the ancient university city, dominated by its cathedral and castle. The platforms are wide, with ample awnings, and the buildings are in a Tudor-Gothic style. The city of Durham is described in detail on page 57.

As we leave Durham station there are more superb views across the city before we run for a few more miles through undulating countryside to Chester-le-Street, a busy market town to the east of the line, dominated by the slender spire of its church. We can enjoy more good views of the town from the viaduct carrying the railway above the streets. The fourteenth-century Lumley Castle can be seen just to the south of the town, while on the high land to the east is the eighteenth-century Lambton Castle. Although Chester-le-Street has a population of 21,000, no long-distance trains stop there, so visitors generally have to change to a local diesel multiple unit train at either Durham or Newcastle.

Just to the north is Birtley Junction, where the remains of the branch to Consett trail in from the west. In the early 1980s, a determined local campaign was mounted to reopen this line for passengers, but Durham County Council did not see fit to back it financially, and the closure of Consett steelworks meant the end of this railway. It could have served Beamish with its famous Open Air Museum. This can now be reached by a half-hourly bus service from Newcastle, dropping passengers three-quarters of a mile from the museum. The museum is described on page 42.

Soon we reach the start of the Tyneside conurbation. Tyne Marshalling Yard is passed on the west, then the Team Valley opens out with its vast trading estate, built in the 1930s. The Tyne Valley is then before us, with factories, houses and tower blocks all around. The line from Carlisle burrows underneath and joins the main line as the centre of Newcastle swings into view: a solid handsome city on the banks of the Tyne. The six remarkable bridges which cross the river in its steep-sided valley here each contribute to the character of the North East's capital.

Most trains from the south cross the Tyne on King Edward Bridge, which was opened in 1906 and whose sturdy arches carry four rail tracks. Other trains run further east past Gateshead diesel depot, over the older High Level Bridge designed by Robert Stephenson with two rail tracks on its upper deck and a roadway underneath. Once over the Tyne, trains come to a halt at one of the curving platforms in Newcastle Central, which, like York and Darlington stations further south, is a massive structure with all the facilities you would expect in a major InterCity station. Newcastle is described on page 58.

The journey northwards from Newcastle may be by Edinburgh-bound High Speed Train, or by one of the few remaining local services using the East Coast Main Line. For diesel multiple units also make a dozen trips up the line, mostly as far as Morpeth but some as far as Alnmouth, serving five other small stations *en route*. Thus you can enjoy a more leisurely ride up to the Northumberland coast, using the smaller stations as starting points for exploring the area by bicycle and, in some instances, by bus.

Your train heads eastwards, with good views of the city centre and the cathedral, through the unstaffed Manors station (less important since the building of the Metro and now only served by a handful of trains). It then veers round in a more northerly direction, passing Heaton depot on the right, opened in 1977 to service both High Speed Trains and diesel multiple units. Soon we are hurrying through the outer suburbs, across a plateau occasionally punctuated by wooded gorges, or denes, cut by small rivers and streams.

Cramlington, 10 miles from Newcastle, is a neat little station built to serve a pleasant village half a mile to the east, which in recent years has been tastefully absorbed by a new town. The residential estates, with their wide roads and spacious lawns, can be seen towards the end of the line, while Cramlington's light industry is located to the west. Buses link Cramlington station to various parts of the new town.

The well-kept station of Morpeth, with its mock-Tudor stone buildings, 6½ miles further on, is approached on a sharp curve, with the main part of this bustling market town picturesquely situated to the north-east of the station, in the wooded valley of the River Wansbeck. It is now the county town of Northumberland, with a population of 14,000, and its places of interest include a fine large fourteenth-century church, castle ruins, a nineteenth-century bridge designed by Thomas Telford and the remains of a medieval one, an unusual clock tower, and an imposing eighteenth-century town hall. There is also a pleasant park, and walks by the river.

Our trains crosses the valley on a nine-arch viaduct to the east of the town and soon reaches Pegswood – two platforms with a metal shelter on one of them, in a cutting on the edge of the village. A mile down the road is picturesque Bothal, on the banks of the Wansbeck, with its castle.

The line curves northwards again, into open country. A few miles to the east we can see two rows of chimneys belonging to the aluminium works at Lynemouth and a freight line heads off towards the coastal collieries. But now we have left industry largely behind, with just a few villages and open-cast coal-mines punctuating the coastal plain of arable land.

Widdrington station is still open, serving a sizeable residential settlement, and is next to a large social club and Co-op store typical of the North East.

The next station, Acklington, stands in a more isolated position and the main building, in local stone, is fenced off and used as a private residence. To the east is an old airfield, and beyond it an open prison. This station is a useful starting point for cycle trips eastwards along quiet, flat roads to the little port of Amble, or westwards on hillier roads up Coquetdale.

Presently we cross the pretty River Coquet and can see out to sea to Coquet Island. Nearer the line, Warkworth Castle dominates an attractive stone-built village. Warkworth station, like several others on this stretch of line, closed in 1958.

Higher land now closes in from the west and the sea comes clearly into view on the east as we draw into Alnmouth, 34¾ miles from Newcastle. A few High Speed Trains call at Alnmouth station, but some long-distance passengers may wonder why, as they gaze out at open countryside to the west. In fact, this station is an important railhead for the seaside village of Alnmouth, huddled on its promontory a mile to the east, and the ancient borough of Alnwick (pronounced Annick) 3 miles up the valley to the west. The station itself is actually situated in the intervening village of

Hipsburn! Its extensive car park testifies to the station's importance as a railhead, and BR spent £76,000 on new permanent buildings in 1986–7.

There is also an hourly bus service passing the station approach, and another of similar frequency calling at the nearby roundabout, giving remarkably good connections to Alnwick (only ten minutes away) and down the coast to Warkworth and Amble. Cyclists will find it a pleasant ride down to Warkworth and alongside the estuary to Amble, continuing southwards, perhaps, to rejoin the train at one of the stations nearer Newcastle.

The town of Alnwick is well worth a visit. It used to be served by a branch line, and as we enter it on the road from Alnmouth, the station building with its overall roof, now serving as a warehouse, is on the left. It seems palatial for a branch-line terminus, but was no doubt designed to be in keeping with Alnwick Castle, home of the Duke of Northumberland, at the other end of the little town. The castle overlooks a park landscaped by Capability Brown and is open to visitors in the summer. Many pleasant hours can be spent exploring this stone-built market town and its surroundings, which include a medieval gate and priory, a fifteenth-century church and a monument to King Malcolm III of Scotland, slain here in 1093.

Indeed, we are now in country which was the scene of constant conflict between the English and Scots in the Middle Ages. Hence the frequency of castles – the next of which is Dunstanburgh, whose distant ruins on the coast can be seen from the train a few miles further north.

Only one station remains open on the final 32½ miles from Alnmouth to Berwick. This is Chathill, serving an isolated hamlet of half-a-dozen houses and a post office huddled round its stone station house and signal box. Only three up and two down trains per day stop here and in this quiet spot, Kings Cross, or even Newcastle Central, seem a long way away.

Yet here too there is something to see. A mile to the south is Preston Tower – a fascinating fourteenth-century Pele Tower used as a refuge during border raids. Situated in the pleasant grounds of a country house, it is open for most of the year.

A post bus passes this way and also links Chathill station morning and evening to Seahouses, a popular little resort 5 miles away on the coast, once served by a

Newcastle–Berwick stopping service running close to the sea near Tweedmouth (*Photo:* John C. Baker)

light railway (closed in 1951) and from which we can take a boat trip to the Farne Islands.

The land is now quite flat again, and water troughs used to be positioned between the rails just north of here at Lucker, for steam locomotives to replenish themselves when travelling at speed. On a clear day we can see to the north-east Bamburgh Castle, which is still inhabited. Grace Darling, the lighthouse-keeper's daughter and heroine of a daring sea rescue in 1838, is buried in Bamburgh churchyard and there is a Grace Darling museum in the village.

The wooded Cheviot Hills now become more prominent to the west and the Great North Road shares the narrowing coastal plain with the railway. Just across the water to the east is Holy Island, also known as Lindisfarne, dominated by its castle and priory ruins. This was one of the earliest bases of Christianity in the north of England, being settled by Irish monks in AD 634. Visitors to Holy Island can reach it by bus from Berwick-upon-Tweed. The causeway linking the island to the mainland is impassable at high tide, so, when planning a trip there, you must consult the local tide table as well as the timetable!

As our train continues northwards on its final leg to the border, you may spot the narrow tower of Haggerston Castle in the trees to the left. However your gaze will probably be drawn more to the right as we now run close to the rocky shore for a few miles before bearing inland. After climbing round on an embankment behind the houses of Tweedmouth, we strike across the valley and the Tweed estuary on the Royal Border Bridge, a graceful twenty-eight-arch viaduct designed by Robert Stephenson and opened by Queen Victoria in 1850.

Immediately beyond the bridge is Berwick-upon-Tweed station, its single island platform built on the site of the former royal castle, part of whose outer walls can be seen to the west. Berwick, the most northerly town in England, is described on page 62. All but the fastest long-distance trains call here before crossing the border and commencing the final scenic leg to the Scottish capital.

After leaving Berwick, our train soon regains the coast and hugs the clifftop for 5 scenic miles, passing on its way the large trackside sign marking the Scottish border. Passing the fishing village of Burnmouth, the line then swings sharply inland and we travel through the rich agricultural Merse of Berwickshire to the small market town of Reston. There are no stations left on this stretch: they succumbed to the Beeching axe of the 1960s.

The line follows the valley of the Eye Water up to Grantshouse, and then comes a cutting through which the line was diverted after the collapse of the adjacent Penmanshiel Tunnel in March 1979. This accident, in which two men died, occurred during excavation work to lower the tracks (as was done successfully in two tunnels further south), so that larger Freightliner trains could be accommodated.

Soon we pass the small village of Cockburnspath and enjoy a further scenic 5-mile run along the coast, punctuated by Torness nuclear power station, before the descent to Dunbar. InterCity trains still call at this historic and popular resort, with its small fishing harbour, ruined castle and John Muir Country Park.

Now the scenery changes again, as we turn inland across rich farming country, the northern horizon dominated by the summit of North Berwick Law. Soon the branch line from North Berwick trails in from the right and we pass the little station of Drem, now served only by local trains.

The next station, Longniddry, serves a large dormitory village on the shores of the Firth of Forth, and is followed by Prestonpans and Musselburgh, the latter station reopened in 1988 to serve the growing commuter traffic. We have now reached the suburbs of Edinburgh, and our train soon pulls into the grand Waverley station, in the heart of the Scottish capital.

The city of Edinburgh and all the rail routes from it are described in detail in our companion volume *Scotland by Rail*. Electrification to Edinburgh is due for completion in May 1991. Our electric train terminates here, but frequent diesel trains will convey you onward to Glasgow, Stirling, Dundee and Aberdeen. The Railway Development Society, and many other bodies in Scotland, will be pressing for the extension of electrification over these routes during the 1990s.

DARLINGTON–BISHOP AUCKLAND: THE 'HERITAGE LINE'
by Marc Lewis

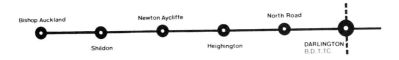

The name 'Heritage Line' was adopted in the 1980s and is an appropriate one for the route to Bishop Auckland, most of which dates from the building of the original Stockton & Darlington Railway in 1825.

To reach North Road Station Railway Museum, one can either take a bus, or walk the mile from the town centre, passing on the way the site of Northgate House where George Stephenson worked on the planning and construction of the line.

Alternatively there is the hourly Paytrain service to Bishop Auckland from Bank Top, which heads north on the main line, past the former motive power depot, to Parkgate Junction. Here the Bishop Auckland line swings to the north-west and joins the route of the Stockton & Darlington Railway coming in from the east, on its now largely abandoned original course from Oak Tree Junction on the Saltburn line.

The railway then crosses the River Skerne on the celebrated bridge built by James Bonomi of Durham, and immortalised in Dobbin's famous painting, *The Opening of the Stockton & Darlington Railway, 1825*. Those who know the painting will observe that the surroundings now are somewhat less rural than they were! Just before passing over North Road Bridge, we see to the south the site of the now-demolished goods warehouse, which housed the world's first ticket office until the present station was opened in 1841.

The British Rail portion of the North Road Station consists of a single platform covered by the typical North Eastern Railway overall roof. The museum incorporates the other half of the island platform as well as the original station buildings, which were renovated in time to be officially opened by Prince Philip on 27 September 1975 – the 150th anniversary of the opening of the S&DR.

Darlington Railway Museum contains a fascinating collection of both small and large items relating to the establishment, development, contraction and modernisation of railways in the North East. Without doubt, pride of place belongs to the largest exhibits from the Stockton & Darlington Railway, first among which is the internationally-famous *Locomotion*. This engine hauled the first S&DR train from Shildon to Stockton at an average speed of 8 mph, no mean feat considering that the twenty-one coal wagons and passenger coach forming the train may have had a load of over 500 people!

The excellent official guide to the museum also gives a brief but cogent account of the development and decline of the railway system around Darlington. At the time of writing, opening times for the museum are 1000–1600, Monday to Saturday and 1400–1600 on Sundays, from the beginning of April to the end of September. The museum can be telephoned on Darlington 460532. Adjacent are the premises of the Darlington Railway Preservation Society, which has a small but growing collection of locomotives and is in the course of establishing a Darlington Railway Centre.

The Bishop Auckland train continues north-west past the works of Whessoe Engineering Ltd. This firm was founded by Alfred and William Kitching, who were responsible for building the locomotive *Derwent* in 1845. The design was intended for working over sharply curved colliery lines, while being powerful enough to haul a worthwhile payload on the Stockton–Darlington main line, and was the successful predecessor of a number of similar engines. *Derwent* can be seen in the North Road Museum.

To the right is a very large area of derelict land which used to contain the North Road Locomotive Shops, closed in 1966 after an illustrious history of over 100 years. Part of the site along the frontage of North Road is now occupied by a large branch of the Morrison's supermarket chain, on the front of which can be seen the old works' clock.

To the left after Whessoe's is Hopetown Junction and the short freight line which used to continue to Barnard Castle and Middleton-in-Teesdale, or westward over the notoriously wild Stainmore summit, to Tebay and Penrith on the West Coast Main Line. Today the branch connects the terminals of UKF Fertilisers and Whessoe Ltd. with the Railfreight network.

The train now heads out into pleasant open country on a straight and evenly graded alignment, which demonstrates well George Stephenson's policy of providing an easy road for the small, not very powerful engines of his time. The next stop is Heighington (over a mile from the pretty village of that name), where *Locomotion* was first placed on rails and steamed, after its difficult road journey from Newcastle where it was built. The cobbled section of the low platform by the original station building is believed to date from the 1830s when regular steam-hauled passenger trains were introduced.

At Heighington we are on the southern limit of Newton Aycliffe, which was developed during the post-war period to provide a greater diversity of industry in the area. It was one of the smaller new towns, having a population target of only 10,000, later increased to 45,000. New towns have not been as successful in the north as in the south – a fact that may be due to the strength of the community feeling in already established areas, as much as to the failure to attract new industry and poor public transport links in an area of low car ownership. Although the railway passes along the southern perimeter of Newton Aycliffe, its station was not opened until 1 January 1978, and certain other new towns in the North East, such as Peterlee and Washington, are still dependent on bus services.

Just before Newton Aycliffe station is the site of Simpasture Junction, generally thought to be the first railway junction between two rival companies. The Clarence Railway provided a rather more direct route to the River Tees at Port Clarence near Billingham, and caused the Stockton & Darlington more than a little alarm. In 1915, the North Eastern Railway electrified the line from Shildon sidings to Tees Yard (between Thornaby and Middlesbrough) on the 1,500 volt overhead system, which proved so successful that the company prepared an abortive scheme to electrify the main line from York to Newcastle – now to be realised as part of the London–Leeds/Edinburgh electrification by British Rail in 1991!

On leaving Newton Aycliffe, another straight stretch takes us to Shildon, for many years the motive power headquarters of the Stockton & Darlington. British Rail Engineering Limited closed the wagon works in the summer of 1984, thus depriving the town of its main employer. The fleet of large 'HAA' wagons used in 'merry-go-round' coal trains were constructed in the works situated on a branch to the west of the Bishop Auckland line. This point was also marked the western limit of locomotive haulage on the Stockton & Darlington. Beyond here the railway ascended and descended Brusselton Hill into the valley of the River Gaunless (a tributary of the Wear) by means of a double incline, and horses would take trains through West Auckland to the foot of Etherley Incline from where they were raised and then lowered into Weardale at Witton Park Colliery, which was the original objective of the Stockton & Darlington Railway. Five years after the railway opened, a branch was built from West Auckland up the Gaunless Valley to Haggerleases to tap the collieries there.

At Shildon the Timothy Hackworth Museum (open April–September) celebrates the life and times of the Stockton & Darlington's first Mechanical Engineer. The engine-shed contains a working replica of Hackworth's engine *Sans Pareil*, which was an unsuccessful competitor against Stephenson's *Rocket* at the Liverpool & Manchester Railway's Rainhill Trials, held in 1829 to determine the best type of locomotive for the world's first inter-city railway. The more energetic visitor may walk to the top of Brusselton Incline, but good boots and outdoor clothes are highly advisable.

After Shildon station the line plunges into a tunnel, after passing on the left the junction site of the former Black Boy Incline Branch, built in 1827 to connect the collieries in the Coundon area. Shildon Hill proved to be a great obstacle to extending rail services to Bishop Auckland, and the tunnel was not opened until 1842 at a cost of £100,000. Even then, the line terminated at South Church until the viaduct across the River Gaunless could be built.

The opening to Bishop Auckland in 1845 enabled direct lines to replace the Brusselton, Etherley and Black Boy inclines and allowed locomotive working throughout the Stockton & Darlington. Clearing Shildon Tunnel we soon run into Bishop Auckland station, relocated on the old Stockton & Darlington platform in June 1986. The rest of what used to be a very extensive station site is now occupied by car-parking, a road by-pass and a supermarket development. The remaining platform holds a modern single-storey building.

Since 1983, the Bishop Auckland line and its Weardale extension to Stanhope has been promoted as the 'Heritage Line' because of its associations with the Stockton & Darlington Railway. It has also been the subject of a scheme to encourage community involvement in the running of local routes, between BR and the County Council, Aycliffe Development Corporation, Darlington Borough and Sedgefield and Wear Valley District Councils.

The attractive villages of the Wear Valley are all accessible by bus, although services may not be frequent, and visitors are advised to consult the Durham County Council *Tourist Travel Guide* (see Further Information section).

'Bishop', as it is known locally, was something of a boom town during the industrial revolution, although now regrettably suffering like the rest of this part of County Durham from an unemployment rate considerably above the national average. The town is still the principal service and shopping centre for the surrounding district, and has a large market square with an interesting Franco-Gothic Town Hall, opened in 1861.

Bishop Auckland's main attraction is Auckland Castle, which has been the official residence of the Bishop of Durham since Norman times. The superb seventh-century private chapel was built from the ruins of a medieval Banqueting Hall and is open at certain times to the public (check with the Tourist Information Office). The Bishop's Park is open during daylight hours. One mile from town to the north is Binchester and its Roman fort, Vinovia. The fort contains the best example of a Roman military bath house in Britain. For opening times telephone Bishop Auckland 663089.

WEAR VALLEY LINE

(Sunday service only)

by Geoffrey Longstaff

When the last passenger train passed through Stanhope on 29 June 1953 it seemed to be the end of the 91-year-long rail connection between Weardale in West Durham and the main rail network. However, in 1988 the contact was partially re-established, with the introduction of two return-services each summer Sunday from the regular passenger terminus at Bishop Auckland.

This service has gradually improved and there are plans for four extensions of the normal Heritage Line journey in the summer of 1990. Furthermore, the overall season for the Stanhope line has been extended and trains are now available between March and the end of October, the route now being traversed by modern Pacer units.

A great deal of credit for the reinstatement of this lies with local authorities in the area, who see the service as an all-purpose line and not solely catering for the tourist industry. As proof of their commitment to the route, the county and district councils have contributed £9,000 to infrastructure work at Stanhope station. This financial collaboration with British Rail's Provincial Sector will continue throughout 1990.

Surprisingly, the Bishop Auckland station and track remodelling left no crossing-point between the track adjoining the platform and the branch line itself. Therefore, the train picks its passengers up and reverses back towards Shildon until a crossing-point is obtained, and then proceeds back under the road bridge and past the station. The train now commences its 16-mile trip at a leisurely pace, taking nearly an hour to complete the single-line route.

As the train leaves the cuttings behind, it is possible to look back over the valley and glimpse Newton Cap Viaduct stretching over the River Wear. This viaduct once carried the rail service from Bishop Auckland to Durham and Newcastle. The route we are following passes near the village of Escomb and its historic seventh-century Saxon church, and then quickly reaches the station of Etherley (actually in the village of Witton Park). The platform and extensive station buildings survive and old sidings can be noted on the right side. These lead into an old BR disposal site which is now closed.

We now bend to the north and cross over the Wear by the viaduct where it is possible to discern the site of Wear Valley Junction and the old line trailing away further northwards toward Crook. As the train curves sharply to the west again a Conservation Trust Nature Reserve dominates the view to the left.

Four miles out of Bishop Auckland, the train passes by the village of Witton-le-Wear and crosses the A68. This was also a halt in previous times, and nearby is the pleasantly sited fifteenth-century Witton Castle and its associated leisure centre.

Turning north again the route becomes a close-running companion of the River Wear all the way to Stanhope. The countryside is now very pleasant with river and woods to the left and more open farming land to the right. The long-neglected platform is visible in the trees at Harperley, situated between the line and the river.

After 10 miles we reach Wolsingham, the gateway to Weardale. This small town is situated in a good walking area, especially around Tunstall Reservoir. Watch out for the sturdy stone station on the right which is in use as a private residence. The line is now in an Area of Outstanding Natural Beauty and lies to the south of the river.

Another 3 miles brings the route to Frosterley, famous for Frosterley Marble, a beautiful form of limestone which was used in the creation of many fonts, pillars and memorials throughout Durham. Examples are also to be found in Durham Cathedral and Auckland Palace Chapel. The platform and station building still exist, again the latter being occupied. Frosterley marked the original terminus of this part of the Wear Valley Railway when this section opened in 1847. The extension to Stanhope arrived fifteen years later.

As the line continues to bridge the river, the train, now deep in the valley, arrives at its destination: 'the capital of Weardale', Stanhope. Both platforms still exist, but passengers alight on the 'up' side. A NER 'Meccano' bridge allows people to cross to the far platform although the town is situated to the north of the station. A small shop and café have opened up in the railway buildings.

Stanhope is surrounded by high fells, reaching up to 2,000 feet in height to the south-west. There are many local beauty spots and the town contains a mock medieval castle, Stanhope Hall (a fortified manor house) and St Thomas's church which has within its ground a famous fossil tree which is 250 million years old.

The small town centre is about five minutes' walk from the rail station or can be reached by a connecting bus service. The same service also provides a spectacular trip higher up the dale and over into Cumbria. Possible stopping-off points include the Weardale Museum at Ireshopeburn (tel. Weardale (0388) 537417) ; the remote Killhope Wheel Lead Mining Centre, Britain's best preserved lead mining site (tel. Durham (091) 386 4411 ext. 2354, or Weardale 537505) and Alston. This town is the home of the narrow-gauge South Tynedale Railway. Details of connecting bus times and special fares for rail users can be obtained from Weardale Motor Services (tel. Weardale 528235). Another regular bus service operates back along the valley to Bishop Auckland, allowing passengers to explore areas passed through on the train.

The Wear Valley line actually runs beyond Stanhope up to Eastgate, 3 miles further on. Here lies the main purpose for retaining the route since its original closure to passengers, the Blue Circle Cement Works. About 300,000 tonnes per annum are transported by rail from Eastgate to Darlington and beyond. The works can be seen on the bus journey to Alston, as can the route of the abandoned section of the line which finally terminated at Wearhead, 25 miles from Bishop Auckland.

The future
Durham County Council supports moves towards running trains on Saturdays, but this step would cause problems in finding times for outbound trains from Darlington running all the way to Stanhope. BR also state it would be difficult to find spare units and drivers, but such services could provide a relief facility for the regular Heritage Line trains. They could also give the people of the dale easy access to shops and amenities in Darlington and Cleveland. The ultimate objective of full reinstatement would lead to vastly increased overall costs, but a feasibility study is being conducted. The Friends of the Heritage Line is a pressure group that has been formed to pursue improvements to the service.

The possibility of opening the intermediate stations has also been looked at, but this would require expensive repair work to platforms and track, a feature that a more regular service would make justifiable. The owners of the properties would also have to provide their consent.

However, while the cement works remain open, the future is assured. Further developments near the line include a Dales Skill Centre in Stanhope, and the planning of an Alpine Leisure Village near Wolsingham.

The line obviously has an important role to play in the future economic development of County Durham, but the railway must be properly equipped to meet all needs, placing the emphasis on greater investment in the line and its infrastructure.

DARLINGTON–SALTBURN

by Stephen Benyon

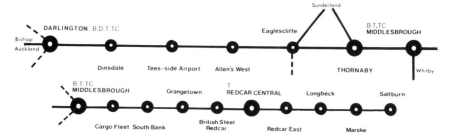

Darlington Bank Top Station was designed by the North Eastern Railway architect, William Bell, and completed in 1887. Many consider it to be his finest creation.

Its triple-span roof is 1,000 feet long and covers a large island platform, with the station offices along its centre. The imposing main entrance with its lofty clock tower is on the western side facing the town, but this has never proved as popular as the side carriage road that leads up to the concourse at the northern end.

In the mid-1980s, a £1.2 million renovation scheme was carried out with steelwork, glazing, timber and slating all being repaired. A complete repainting of the building included some nicely picked out ironwork. Train information monitors were installed, and in 1989 a further £129,000 was spent on new platform surfaces, flower-beds and floodlighting. The station is once again a credit to the town.

Pride of place on the timetable of course goes to the InterCity service, but at one time many of Darlington's departures ran to the east and west. Now there are only two such branches left: Bishop Auckland to the north-west and Saltburn to the east, with infrequent additional trains to Hartlepool.

Through-trains from Bishop Auckland to Saltburn use platform 1, while those originating at Darlington use the south bay, platform 2. The weekday service is still basically a half-hour one, just as it was forty years ago, and is run by modern Pacer units. The journey of 27¾ miles takes just under an hour and provides the traveller with a wide variety of views, from open country and glimpses of the sea, to the stark industrial landscape of Teesside.

Several of the intermediate stations make good starting points for further exploration into Cleveland and North Yorkshire. This route is also of great historical interest, for it utilises much of the original Stockton & Darlington Railway main line.

A well-known local landmark on the other side of the main line as the train leaves, is the giant thermometer erected at the works of W. Richardson & Co., Heating Engineers, during the early 1950s, and recently returned to working order. The Richardson works and the neighbouring Cleveland Bridge and engineering factory have all been demolished to clear the railside down to Thompson Street bridge.

After crossing the East Coast Main Line, the train rounds Geneva Curve and heads eastward past Eastbourne and Firth Moor housing estates. This section of track was specifically built to allow trains to use the south end of Bank Top station. A shallow cutting leads the line under the A66, into open country and to Dinsdale: the first stop. Less than a mile to the south of the station, beyond the village of Middleton St George, the River Tees can be found meandering through an attractive gorge. From here, the more adventurous traveller can continue further along peaceful country roads into rural North Yorkshire. After another half mile, at Oak Tree Junction, the train takes the course of the 1825 S&D Railway which curves in from the left, and we are travelling on the most famous railway in the world.

After crossing the Yarm road at Goosepool, the line runs along the northern perimeter of Teesside Airport, built in the early war years as RAF Middleton St George. This aerodrome now sees a third of a million passengers a year, and since 1971 has had its own interchange station. The LNER 1925 centenary procession was held on this stretch and the grandstand stood on the northern side, where the road swings slightly away from the railway for about 400 yards. A new bridge allows the Yarm road to pass under the railway, avoiding Urlay Nook level-crossing, which, however, has to remain in use to serve the road to Long Newton and the nearby British Chrome & Chemical Works – a first taste of Teesside industry. Eaglescliffe Naval Stores Depot is then seen over on the left, shortly before the next station, Allens West, built in 1943 as a workmen's halt but now open to the public. A branch opened in October 1825 went off to Yarm from here to supply coal and lime depots, and its course can be discerned by a line of bushes curving away to the right.

The line then turns northward, joining the 1852 Leeds Northern route which comes in from Northallerton on the right, and the train stops at the formerly very busy interchange station of Eaglescliffe. Two inland platforms and an extensive range of buildings once existed here, but these became very dilapidated in later years and it is said that the last straw came when the ceiling collapsed over the 'ladies' while it was occupied by a booking clerk. The lady was thankfully unhurt, but the buildings had to go, and by 1970 accommodation had been reduced to a basic level.

Half an hour's walk away or a short bus ride to the south of Eaglescliffe, by the River Tees, lies the delightful town of Yarm with its broad and graceful Georgian street. Some of the inns still have archways which led to stables in coaching days, and it is one of these inns, the George and Dragon, which bears evidence of Yarm's particular association with the S&D Railway: a plaque to commemorate the promoters' meeting held there on 20 February 1820. Completely straddling the west side of the town is a magnificent viaduct which carries the Eaglescliffe–Northallerton line. It is almost half a mile long and contains seven million bricks.

A quarter of a mile to the north of Eaglescliffe station, on the east side of the Stockton road, stands Preston Hall, one of the finest Victorian social history museums in the country. Set in large picturesque grounds, it features an open-air period street and houses a fine collection of arms and armour, a large collection of early silver, period rooms, a small toy museum, and Georges de la Tour's famous painting, *The Dice Players*, which was found some years ago in the attic! More traces of the original S&D Railway can be found in the grounds, in the form of a low tree-grown embankment.

After a mile of running northwards the train turns eastwards again, leaving the route to Stockton behind. On the left are the remains of the once electrified mineral line from Shildon, and at Bowesfield Junction is the now closed NER line of 1877 from Redmarshall. Also on the left and still surviving is the curve from Hartburn Junction which allows traffic to run direct from Stockton to Middlesbrough. No wonder Bowesfield was one of the busiest junctions on the LNER, for most of Teesside's railborne traffic comes through here.

Following this, the remains of another section of the 1825 line can be seen branching off to the left. This originally ran down to Stockton Quay where coal was shipped and the passenger coaches stopped. The original ticket office is still standing and can be reached from Bridge Road.

The train rumbles across the girder bridge over the Tees, with the town of Stockton on the left, before calling at Thornaby, another interchange station. Here again is an island platform where impressive but redundant buildings have been replaced by a more functional, if spartan, brick shelter.

The line now skirts round Thornaby Motive Power Depot and the large complex of sidings which form the Tees Marshalling Yard. Over to the right, on the other side of the Stockton–Middlesbrough road, extensive construction work is now going on with the building of Tees Park shopping and leisure complex. Disappointingly, a new rail halt is not at present being considered to serve this, as was done at the very popular Gateshead Metro Centre.

This stretch of passenger line is crossed by two footbridges, the second of which was transported from Cockfield station when the Barnard Castle–Bishop Auckland branch closed. The huge Tees Bridge carrying the A19 looms overhead, and the train then passes under the southern approach road to the Newport Lift Bridge, opened on 28 February 1934 by the then Duke of York. This bridge was the first of its kind in England and is still the largest in existence.

Far over to the left can be seen the huge Billingham ICI complex, and between the railway and the river, a pleasantly landscaped stretch of ground. This was the Ironmasters district of Middlesbrough, and the name is now the only obvious evidence of the works and cramped rows of back-to-back houses that once hemmed in the railway. After a brief glimpse of Transporter Bridge, the line curves round into platform 2 of Middlesbrough station.

In 1821 a census recorded a total of five families at Middlesbrough, each mainly employed in agriculture, and the place was described as little more than a swamp with a few farm buildings. But seven years later the Stockton & Darlington Railway Company decided to build coal shipping staiths here, where the River Tees is deeper, and modern Middlesbrough was founded. It is now a town of 150,000 people and is at the heart of one of Britain's leading industrial centres. It is the commercial, shopping and entertainment centre of Cleveland county.

Any appraisal is incomplete, however, without mention of the area's most famous son, the navigator, James Cook, who was born in the village of Marton on 27 October 1728. To honour him, a fine purpose-built museum has been established in Middlesbrough's Stewart Park.

The present station was opened in 1877, and has an impressive Gothic façade approached by a long carriage ramp, but the loss of its overall roof following a German daylight raid on 3 August 1942 has radically changed its appearance. During the two days the station was out of use, United buses replaced some trains and were in the charge of LNER guards, complete with whistles and green flags. Two features that have survived are a very good example of an NER tile map on platform 2, and the ornate Albert Bridge, beneath the east end of the station. The platforms and booking hall have been smartened up considerably in recent years, and the buffet, now called 'Chuffers', is strongly recommended for its excellent standards of food and service.

As the train leaves, Transporter Bridge comes into view again to the left, spanning the Tees. Built in 1911 to link Middlesbrough with Port Clarence and destined to become the town's most famous landmark, it is the only one of its kind still working in the country. The Whitby branch swings away to the right, while closer views of river activity are available to the left. East of Middlesbrough station, through Cargo Fleet, South Bank and Grangetown and almost to Redcar, there were ironworks, steelworks and blast furnaces, each with its own sidings and fleet of locomotives for internal shunting. But the trend to move downriver continues, and much of the industry now occupies more spacious sites nearer the mouth of the Tees. A new halt was opened in 1978 to serve the recently-completed Redcar works of the British Steel Corporation.

Earlier maps show the railway running quite close to the river, for the Tees basin was once wide and shallow, but nearly all the land to the left has since been reclaimed so the scene has changed completely. In the distance to the right are the Eston Hills, and sprawling before them the huge ICI Wilton Works, where thanks to the generosity of the company, A2 Pacific *Blue Peter* is undergoing restoration at No.9 depot.

Despite the close proximity of heavy industry, Redcar still manages to maintain its air of a holiday resort, with miles of sands, sea-front entertainments, a large indoor

Transporter Bridge – the symbol of Middlesbrough (*Photo:* Stephen Benyon)

fun-fair and a racecourse. There is also a very good folk festival held there in July. A summer Saturday will find train-loads of people getting out for a good old-fashioned day by the sea. The beach is a mere seven minutes' walk down Station Road, while the racecourse is a few minutes away in the opposite direction.

The station still retains its overall roof and was given an additional platform for Middlesbrough-bound trains in 1935. This now features a new booking office and waiting-room, as the old buildings are closed up.

A mile further on is Redcar East, making one aware that the town also supports quite a large residential population, and then comes Longbeck, a new halt opened in the summer of 1985. The hills to the south now come closer as the train calls at Marske before running into Saltburn, terminus of the passenger service. A freight line trails off to the right, running along what is left of the coast route to Whitby, to Boulby potash mine a few miles away.

The Darlington service now uses an uncovered island platform; the original roofed portion opened in 1861 having been removed and a food market built on the site. The impressive yellow brick frontage survives, however, and the buildings have been carefully restored and converted into shops. Traces of the platform and track, which once gave access to the railway-owned Zetland Hotel, are still evident, although now bisected by a path joining the two sides of the town.

An interesting piece of railway history can also be found in the Valley Gardens, where the stone portico from old Barnard Castle station, which closed as long ago as 1862, stands. Purchased the following year by the Saltburn Improvement Company, it was dismantled and transported forty miles to the coast.

Saltburn is a quiet Victorian resort, which never realised its potential. The steep walk up from the fine sandy beach can be avoided by using the funicular railway lift. There is a pier, though unfortunately the end section was washed away in a storm some fourteen years ago. In August there are Victorian celebrations with bunting, fancy dress, a steam locomotive from the North York Moors Railway, and train rides to Boulby.

From the foot of the wooded gorge of Skelton Beck, by the beach, energetic walkers can make a start on the Cleveland Way, which follows the spectacular coast to Whitby and utilises some of the trackbed of the Whitby, Redcar & Middlesbrough Union Railway.

MIDDLESBROUGH–WHITBY
by Stephen Benyon and Meg Iredale

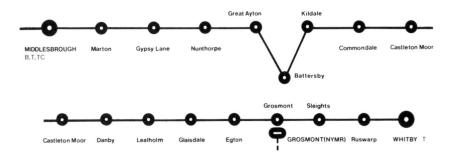

Between the North Yorkshire coastline and the Vale of York lie the North Yorkshire Moors: bounded to the west by the steep scarp of the Hambleton Hills and to the north-west by the Cleveland Hills. Now designated a National Park, this area of rugged moorland and beautiful secluded valleys covers 553 square miles and is virtually unspoilt.

The moors are mainly composed of sandstone, and the heather blooms magnificently from mid-summer to autumn. This is fine walking country with routes like the Cleveland Way, the White Rose Walk, the Captain Cook Trail and the well-known Lyke Wake Walk offering challenges for the more energetic. Many visitors though, will be content to enjoy the scenic splendours of the countryside, and to explore stone-built villages and market towns such as Castleton, Lealholm, Goathland and Helmsley.

Through this scenery runs the Middlesbrough-Whitby railway: the Esk Valley line, following the course of Yorkshire's only salmon river down to the sea. Never conceived as a complete route, but formed of remaining sections of separate lines built for differing reasons, this railway has survived a number of closure threats and now seems to have a fairly well assured future.

It is still the only means of transport for many people living in the valley, and carries a considerable number of schoolchildren to and from Whitby each day. In summer, receipts are swelled by large numbers of walkers bound for the moors, and people heading for a pleasant day at the seaside.

The 35-mile journey begins at Middlesbrough, platform 2. There are seven trains each way, with six more going as far as Nunthorpe, and a summer Sunday service. All services are now in the hands of 'Pacer' units. The Esk Valley line has often been associated with this type of lightweight train: before 1914 'steam autocars' worked some services between Stockton and Whitby, and later, six cylinder 'Sentinel' steam railcars came into use, lasting into the 1940s.

East of Middlesbrough, the train leaves the Saltburn line at Guisborough Junction, and enters part of a route opened to passengers by the Middlesbrough & Guisborough Railway in 1854, but built with the object of gaining access to ironstone deposits in the north of the Cleveland Hills. It was the discovery of this mineral which led to the clamorous growth of Teesside industry.

To leave the Tees Valley, trains on this stretch are faced with a long arduous climb of 1½ miles at 1 in 40 from Ormesby to Nunthorpe. A new halt, Gypsy Lane, has also been built on this track to serve a housing development.

At Nunthorpe a single line token is collected and connecting buses run to and from Guisborough, making this quite a busy little station. A mile further on is the site of Nunthorpe Junction, where the train swings southward, leaving the remaining empty trackbed to Guisborough behind. During the 1970s, proposals were made to reopen the 4-mile link to this attractive market town, where substantial housing developments have taken place, but sadly these came to nothing.

The next 5¼-mile-long section from Nunthorpe to Battersby was built by the North Yorkshire & Cleveland Railway and opened to freight traffic in 1864. Also designed as a link with mines and quarries, it was not opened for passengers until 1 April 1868. The pretty village of Great Ayton with its prominent church spire can be seen to the right as the train approaches its station. To the left, high up on Easby Moor, stands Captain Cook's monument. The famous explorer lived and went to school in the village and in the churchyard is a tombstone marking the grave of his mother and five brothers and sisters. Also, towering 1,000 feet above Great Ayton to the north-east is the strange conical hill, Roseberry Topping.

At Battersby the train runs into the station and then reverses on to another track, much to the consternation of first-time travellers. The reason for the apparent anomaly is that Battersby was once a junction. The route from here to Whitby originally started at Picton (between Northallerton and Eaglescliffe), once again under the auspices of the North Yorkshire & Cleveland Railway. Until the closure of the Picton–Battersby secton on 14 June 1954, most Esk Valley trains started their journey at Stockton, with only the occasional Middlesbrough train reversing at Battersby. This junction also connected with a mineral line opened in 1861 to serve ironstone mines in Rosedale, 9 miles to the south-east. This railway ran to the foot of the Cleveland Hills and then up the steep hillside by means of a rope-worked incline nearly a mile long. It then crossed the moors to East and West Rosedale on a line which could be worked by locomotives. Although the last steam engine was lowered down its slopes in June 1929, Ingleby Incline remains a local landmark, and the course of the railway is still visible almost throughout, making it an excellent path for walkers. It now forms part of the Lyke Wake Walk. (To reach the incline from Battersby station, turn left off the road to Ingleby Greenhow.)

With the next single line token collected and the driver seated at the opposite end, the train moves slowly out of Battersby, past the NER pattern water crane and signal cabin, leaving behind a station belonging very much to the past with birch saplings growing where rails once lay.

The line was extended eastwards from here only gradually and opened as far as Castleton in 1861. It now brings the traveller into the North York Moors National Park. Kildale Moor looms up on the right and the train soon draws into Kildale station, with the village church and graveyard close behind the platform. A pleasant 6–10 mile walk can be made from here, through the village and along part of the Cleveland Way to where the Cistercian Nunnery of Baysdale Abbey once stood. You can return by the same route or continue down into the valley, following Baysdale Beck to Castleton station.

Four miles down the line, the station of Commondale also provides a pleasant but shorter walk to Castleton: turn right at 'Oaktrees', the modern bungalow near the station, and follow the farm track. After the railway came to Commondale, a line ⅝-mile long was laid to serve a brick and tile works in the village. The red bricks produced were used in the building of some houses in the area, and these look strangely conspicuous in a district characterised by stone buildings.

After another two miles, Castleton is reached. The village, with tea-room and pubs, stands up on the hillside to the right, and it is from here that the station's picturesque setting is best appreciated. The buildings remain more or less intact, but the empty coal depot and goods yard are a reminder that all freight traffic on this branch has now ceased. Castleton is also another good starting place for walkers, and there are superb panoramic views of this unspoilt country from Castleton Rigg.

Danby is the home of the North York Moors National Park Centre, open daily from

Whitby Abbey ruins

Easter to October, and on winter weekends. It contains an exhibition and information centre on the history, wildlife and making of the moors, as well as helpful guides to walks and picnic places in the area. There are also tea-rooms and a picnic meadow.

Not until the last section of the North Yorkshire & Cleveland Railway from Castleton was opened on 22 October 1865 was it at last possible to run a service the whole length of the Esk Valley, using the Whitby & Pickering Railway between Grosmont and Whitby. The intermediate stations at Danby, Lealholm, Glaisdale and Egton Bridge are all still in fair order, and the attractive two-storey platform buildings are either inhabited or well-used. In common with all Esk Valley stations, they now feature a helpful 'welcome' board showing local walks, sights and news.

Lealholm has some of the valley's loveliest scenery with the river breaking in falls over rocky ledges. The water can be crossed by stepping stones or a 200-year-old stone bridge, and the green is a good place for a picnic.

Glaisdale is probably the most interesting of the group of stations, retaining much of its North Eastern Railway appearance, with an attractive little signal box and weather-boarded waiting shelter. Looking at the village it serves, it is hard to believe that an ironworks and three blast furnaces were kept busy there. The industry was short-lived however, opening in 1866 and lasting only ten years, probably killed off by the competition from Teesside. The slag heaps were eventually sold to Surrey County Council who used the material for road making. Today Glaisdale is better known for an older construction, the Beggars Bridge, built over the Esk in 1619 by one Thomas Ferris, who apparently used to wade across the river to court the squire's daughter. He went away to make his fortune, but finally returned to marry his love and build the bridge.

The river has also caused the railway some problems on this section, where the latter crosses the Esk nine times in 10 miles. On 23 July 1930, torrential rain caused the Esk to flood, and a stone bridge in Arncliff Woods, immediately east of Glaisdale station, was swept away. Three and a half months later the same fate befell its successor and the line was closed for a further twelve months before a third and more substantial double-span bridge could be erected.

After Egton Bridge, home of the World Annual Gooseberry Show every August since 1800, comes Grosmont, a junction with the North Yorkshire Moors Railway, whose carmine and cream coaching stock give the place a very 1950s feel. Here a steam-hauled train can be boarded in the summer for an 18-mile ride over the moors to Pickering. Also from Grosmont there is a pleasant sheltered walk leading to the hills above Goathland. From the station follow the track of George Stephenson's horse-drawn railway, through his original tunnel at Grosmont up to Goathland via Beck Hole. Nearby waterfalls can then be reached by a number of short walks.

For the remaining 6¼ miles to Whitby, the train travels over the oldest section, opened in 1836 as part of the Whitby & Pickering Railway. This was the first passenger-carrying railway in the North Riding of Yorkshire, taking a route chosen by George Stephenson and worked in the beginning by horses. The following stations of Sleights and Ruswarp are distinctive and stepped gable ends of their station houses provide a clue to their separate ancestry.

The railway is now never far from the river, and in the 3¼ miles to Sleights crosses it no less than eight times. Sleights is a greystone village built on a hillside over the Esk and the salmon leap there is one of the valley's real highlights. For those who are too early or late to see the water acrobatics, there is photographic evidence in the Salmon Leap pub.

Approaching Whitby, the huge Larpool Viaduct which carried the now closed line to Scarborough looms ahead. The train rounds a curve on the north side of the river and after passing under a high new road bridge, presents a view of the ruined abbey above the town. After a journey time of one and a half hours, the train finally draws into Whitby Town station, looking decidedly bare with only one platform in use, but still a credit to its staff. Whitby (population 12,000) was once very well served by railways considering its size. By 1895 there were outlets to Malton, Stockton, Saltburn and Scarborough, but it was inevitable that economies would come eventually and by 1965 only the present route remained.

Stepping out of the train you become aware immediately of the sounds and smells of the sea, for Whitby harbour, ringed by a fishing village of steep alleyways and hillside cottages, is only just outside the station. Captain Cook's *Endeavour* was built here and a modern boatyard still builds fishing boats and pleasure craft. In Grape Lane you can stand in the attic where James Cook and his apprentices slept and where he imagined sailing farther than any man had ever sailed before. The Captain Cook Memorial Museum is well worth a visit, as is the 'Dracula Experience', for the evil count was dreamed up by Bram Stoker on a seat by Whitby Abbey. 'Dracula Trail' guides can be picked up from the information centre by the station.

Above the red roofs and steep alleys of Old Whitby stands St Mary's parish church, reached by the renowned 199 steps, while right up on the headland behind it are the jagged sandstone ruins of the Abbey. The first Abbey was founded here by St Hilda in AD 657, but the present building dates from the thirteenth century. Not all of the damage is due to decay however, for in 1914 it was shelled by the German Fleet. West Cliff, on the opposite side of the harbour, forms the more modern seaside resort and has fine sandy beaches.

A spectacular route to a fascinating town, the Esk Valley line offers superb views all the year round. The embankments abound with wild flowers from spring onwards; in autumn the moors glow with heather and bracken; and in winter after snowfall, the whole ride is quite breathtaking.

THE NORTH YORKSHIRE MOORS RAILWAY

by Moira Hunter

As you alight from the BR train at Grosmont's platform 1, there is little today to suggest a busy industrial past. The station yard, once crammed with the wagons of the ironstone industry, now fills with the cars which are the inevitable result of another industry: tourism.

The North Yorkshire Moors Railway is a popular venue for the day-visitor and holidaymaker alike. Over 350,000 passenger journeys are now recorded annually on the line closed by Beeching in the 1960s. Reopened as a charitable trust in 1973, the 18-mile route to Pickering once more sees steam-hauled traffic as well as the many changes needed to build an entire railway from a formerly derelict branch line.

Grosmont can boast two railway tunnels, one of them built for George Stephenson's horse-drawn railway of 1836, and now pedestrian access to the NYMR engine sheds. The repair shed is already too small for the demands of the railway, but engines undergoing maintenance and restoration on the two roads can be seen from the viewing gallery above. On summer mornings, the shed area is bustling with activity as three and possibly four steam locos are prepared for the day's shift.

One of the most gruelling sections of the railway is the first few miles past the hamlet of Esk Valley and up to Goathland, where the 1 in 49 gradient demands much from both crew and loco. Originally the Whitby & Pickering Railway took an easier route along the valley bottom, to meet a steep incline at Beck Hole where wagons were hauled to the top by rope. This hazardous method operated until a fatal accident in 1864 led to the planning of today's deviation route, and the building of Goathland station. However the original route can still be enjoyed today as the Historical Railway Trail.

Goathland station is possibly the most attractive on the line, with a pleasant combination of railway features and a moorland setting. The original NER signal gantry, enamel signs, well-stocked gardens and footbridge (erected in 1986 for the line's 150th anniversary), together with the pastoral surroundings, serve to convince travellers that this is a place where time stands still. Just beyond Goathland however, we are brought very much up-to-date with a brief glimpse of Fylingdales Early Warning Station and its radomes, before plunging into the thick forests of Newtondale. The inaccessibility of this valley prompted the Forestry Commission, North York Moors National Park and Railway to build a simple halt from which three way-marked paths provide an incentive to leave the train awhile. To explore the high ground is to see the North Yorkshire Moors Railway at its best, as the cliffs provide good vantage points for watching the eight-coach trains thunder up the dale. The ruins at Skelton Tower are particularly good for the photographer, and can be reached easily from Levisham station.

The thick forests below Skelton Tower hide quite an industrial heritage. Walker's Pit was the most southerly of the Cleveland ironstone mines, and although its chimney was demolished over a decade ago, remains of cottages and offices can still be found. Raindale Mill – now to be seen working at York Castle Museum – used to sit on the west side of the line, and the privately-owned Grange was an inn in 1836 and a point to provide fresh horses for the railway.

North Yorkshire Moors Railway train leaves Goathland for Pickering (*Photo:* Tom Heavyside)

Levisham station was built to serve the villages of Levisham and Newton-upon-Rawcliffe, and to reach either means quite a walk uphill! The conglomeration of signal box, cottages and station house have made Levisham a very popular film location. Further on at Farwath, a platelayer's cottage is still occupied. Undaunted by the absence of road access, the family there still rely on the train making special stops to take them, and their hand-crafted besoms, to Pickering.

A permanent way yard and signal box at New Bridge herald the approach to Pickering, still over a mile away but reached past carriage sidings holding a vast array of stock: from Gresley coaches built between the wars, to Pullmans in immaculate brown and cream, in regular use on wine-and-dine trains.

Pickering station lost its overall roof many years ago, and the station buildings have seen considerable change in the transition from branch line to tourist attraction. The booking office, parcels office, waiting rooms and news-stand have all disappeared to cater for a different public, and gift shop, tea-room and audio-display area now fit the bill.

The buffer stops stand where previously the line carried on to Rillington Junction, Malton and York, and the former goods yard has been developed into a library, medical centre, and inevitable car park. However signs of the railway's past can still be seen at the Station Master's House, now a good walk away from Pickering station itself.

The buffers may signify the end of the line, but the railway and Pickering town enjoy a new prosperity, and look forward to another 150-year association.

STOCKTON–FERRYHILL

by Peter Walker

The route from Stockton itself is described in the Durham Coast Line chapter, page 28, as far as Norton South signal box. The Ferryhill line leaves the Leeds Northern line here, curves to the left past a garden centre, Blakeston Comprehensive School, and the site of a proposed Co-op SuperStore, and travels through a well-wooded cutting, emerging amid gently-rolling farmland on to a short embankment. Visible in a valley to the right is the village of Thorpe Thewles, once dominated by a large viaduct on a different rail line towards Wellfield, Castle Eden and Ryhope. (A section of that line's trackbed has recently been designated the 'Castle Eden Walkway' and it begins, officially, at a restored Thorpe Thewles railway station, which doubles as a visitor centre, souvenir shop, and museum.) But we dip back into a cutting before threading through Stillington on another embankment. Most of this village, and the more attractive scenery, is on the left: the large Darchem factory occupies most of the outlook on the right. After another short cutting we swing quite sharply to the right, away from the trackbed of the former line towards Newton Aycliffe and Shildon.

Wooded cutting and views over gently undulating country continue to alternate, until a quick succession of overbridges indicates we are passing through Mordon, little of which is visible from the train. After yet another bridge a short way on, we pass the site of Sedgefield station on the right. There is even less of Sedgefield to be seen, despite its growing popularity as a commuter dormitory for Teesside and Darlington, since it is a full 2 miles from the station that once purported to serve it.

By this time, our route is less than a mile east of the East Coast Main Line, and, after a new concrete bridge has carried the A1(M) over our heads, we see the masts of the electric line closing in on our left. The outskirts of Ferryhill Station (a village quite separate from Ferryhill itself!) now indicate that our trip along the goods-only section is almost over. However, in practice, we travel on separate tracks for another mile or so – under the wires, too – before crossing over to the main line proper just before Tursdale.

Interestingly, the parish council of Ferryhill itself (which for these purposes includes the much larger town of Spennymoor) has expressed strong support for a restored Ferryhill station. This would have to be constructed totally from scratch, since there is no sign of the original station that closed in 1967, and among the arguments the councillors are using is the advantage of a direct rail-link with Stockton and Middlesbrough. BR's welcome decision not to abandon Stockton–Ferryhill after all, once full electric services begin via Darlington, gives all in Co. Durham and Cleveland a greater incentive to campaign, with the RDS, for regular passenger services to be restored to this very pleasant stretch of railway.

EAGLESCLIFFE–NORTHALLERTON

by Stephen Benyon

Like the Ferryhill–Stockton line, this is primarily a freight link, but is also used as a diversionary route for InterCity trains when there is engineering work in the Darlington area. It has for some years also carried the 'Cleveland Executive' daily passenger train to and from Kings Cross; but at the time of writing this working is likely to cease. The line does have potential, however, for regular passenger trains from the Teesside conurbation direct to the south.

Opened in 1852 as an extension of the Leeds Northern Railway, this 14¾-mile line is one of the few sections of that railway still in existence. The volume of freight traffic shows little sign of diminishing, for happily most of this is of the type for which rail will always be best suited: coal from the Durham coast collieries; chemicals from the ICI Billingham complex; petroleum and diesel fuel from the Port Clarence and Seal Sands Oil Terminal; and a good percentage of the steel products of Teesside.

The most notable feature of the line is the great brick viaduct at Yarm, which is crossed a few minutes after leaving Eaglescliffe. Almost half a mile long and containing seven million bricks, this magnificent structure completely straddles the western side of the little town.

The rest of the journey, while not so spectacular, is nevertheless very pleasant as the train continues through a warm rural landscape with the great scarp of the Cleveland Hills rising up over to the east.

Eight miles into the journey, the train roars through the level-crossing at Picton. The station is long since closed, but an attractive North Eastern Railway signal box remains manned. Until 1954, Picton was a junction with a line going off eastwards through Stokesley to Battersby (still open on the Whitby branch). Stations also existed once at Welbury and Brompton nearer the end of the line.

There is a good view of the market town of Northallerton to the east, as we curve round into its station on the East Coast Main Line.

Kings Cross–Middlesbrough High Speed Train calls at Eaglescliffe (*Photo:* Tom Heavyside)

DURHAM COAST LINE
by Peter Walker

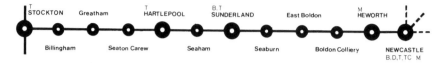

STOCKTON–HARTLEPOOL

Although most passenger trains on this section run to or from Middlesbrough, the Coast Line as such begins at Bowesfield Junction signal box, west of Thornaby station. It curves sharply away from the Darlington–Saltburn route and soon joins the former Leeds Northern line from Northallerton and Eaglescliffe. The lines converge at Hartburn Junction, and after skirting Ropner Park, one of Stockton's more pleasant amenities, the train passes a large scrapyard (with its own shunting locomotives) on the left, and a mixture of twentieth-century and Victorian terraced housing on the right.

Stockton railway station has become an unforgivable eyesore, despite a 10,000-signature petition obtained by local people in an effort to do something about it. The main building on the southbound platform has listed status, but BR closed its ticket office in July 1988. The resulting deterioration and lack of maintenance make it harder than ever to believe that this station is intended to serve the 87,000 inhabitants of one of the towns where railways first began. Even the modest reconstruction of its platforms has, arguably, been botched. Both are now half-length, and too low for modern rolling-stock, whereas a proper full-length reconstruction of the southbound platform alone, plus minor track adjustments of a sort which are planned anyway, could have usefully linked the station with the Durham Road bypass bridge that will shortly straddle the railway line at the north end. In this way, too, the need for the present subway or a future footbridge (also planned) could have been avoided.

Be this as it may, central Stockton itself has much to offer the visitor. The High Street, a short walk away from the station, hosts an extensive street market on Wednesdays, Fridays and Saturdays. The unusual width of this street ensures that even with all the stalls in business, there is still ample room for buses, pedestrians and the occasional car.

A landmark in the High Street is the red-brick eighteenth-century St Thomas's church, thought to have been designed either by Sir Christopher Wren or one of his more promising pupils. The church has recently been extensively redecorated inside, and its old organ replaced by a remarkable instrument that came second-hand from a chapel in Birmingham. It was reassembled by a team of enthusiastic amateurs led by the Vicar of Stockton, himself an accomplished organist and music enthusiast.

Buildings along the middle of the High Street are firstly the Town Hall, recently restored and still housing Stockton District Council's debating chamber, and secondly a building called the 'Shambles' containing part of the indoor market.

Between the High Street and the river, and accessible from both via Finkle Street, is a small and interesting group of buildings in and around Green Dragon Yard, which include a small theatre, some specialist shops and a local museum. For those who have been wondering whereabouts in all this the original Stockton & Darlington Railway premises feature, the answer is that they don't, except for a few museum mentions. The original booking office building is a fair walk beyond the High Street – indeed, it is probably easier to approach it from Thornaby station than from Stockton.

From Stockton station, the line curves left and climbs through the northern out-skirts to Norton South signal box. We slow for a curve away from the direct line towards Ferryhill (described on page 26) and eastwards to the site of the old Norton station, closed in 1959 and dismantled long ago. A level-crossing and a pub (The Norton Tavern) on the right now mark the spot: one of many where county planners would like to build a rail halt if money were available.

Soon we emerge from a shallow cutting on to a new viaduct, then after crossing Billingham Beck and the recently designated 'Country Park', we run under a road bridge that carried the first of Billingham's two attempts at a bypass for the original A19 Stockton–Sunderland road. Passing yet another former station site, that of the original Billingham station, we see a double-track goods line heading eastwards to Billingham's extensive ICI factories, sidings, a former shipyard, Haverton Hill, Port Clarence and Seal Sands. Since just after Norton South Junction, in fact, we have been travelling on what was originally built as the 'Clarence Railway', which explains in part why our route twists and turns so often. The fact is that the present Coast Line was never designed as the main link between Teesside and Wearside, but was grad-ually cobbled together from bits of earlier, more local concerns.

Later in the journey, from Seaham to Sunderland, is the former 'Londonderry Railway' route, but at this point in our journey we content ourselves with turning northwards away from the Port Clarence/ICI branch line and skirting Billingham Town football ground on the right. Passing numerous pigeon lofts on the left, and noting three tall blocks of flats, the upper reaches of Billingham Forum and other landmarks of the town centre in the middle distance beyond them, we sidle under the other main road bridge of the town and into Billingham's 'new' station, an island platform with a brick shelter.

Billingham is a town of some 35,000 people, and its station was deliberately re-sited here in 1966 to serve both the new centre and growing estates to the east. However it always suffered from poor pedestrian access, either by a steep footbridge, or from a 300-yard walk to the nearest road, never mind bus-stop. For the first three years, it had station staff to help passengers over the first difficulty, but the decision to remove them completely in 1969 met with understandable opposition and amaze-ment, especially as Billingham's traffic had been considerably boosted by visitors to the town's Forum, from the Hartlepool direction in particular.

The Forum is a combined indoor sports centre, swimming-pool, skating-rink, bad-minton/squash courts, theatre and restaurants, and one of the first of its kind any-where. It is a short walk from the station and open daily to spectators as well as participants. Its annexe, Forum House, offers simple overnight accommodation at a reasonable price – the nearest such accommodation to the railway, in fact. The Forum complex is still well-used, but visitors travelling by rail to it have decreased now that Hartlepool and Stockton both boast new swimming-pools and other centrally-placed leisure amenities.

The rail line runs absolutely straight for the next 4 miles, through a light industrial estate, sadly not rail-connected, and past Cowpen Bewley village, where the level-crossing was automated a full sixteen years after staff had been removed from Billingham station – an eloquent testimony to the priorities, at that time, of BR management. The flat landscape is broken briefly on the left by the low wooded hill where Greatham village stands. Greatham has a number of noteworthy buildings, including a hospital of historic significance, as well as its parish church, but regret-tably few trains stop at the station despite the efforts of parish councillors and the convenience of its position at the entrance to Rank, Hovis, McDougall's food pro-cessing factory. Instead, most trains hurtle on, past South Durham Iron and Steel Works, happily back in regular production of steel tubes by the train-load after several years' inactivity, and pull up a few minutes later at Seaton Carew.

St Hilda's church, Hartlepool

Few would guess, having just passed a trailing junction with the goods line from Seaton Snook and Hartlepool's nuclear power station visible on the far right, that they have reached one of Cleveland's long-established and, in some ways, very fashionable seaside resorts. But if they are travelling on a warm summer's afternoon, particularly a Sunday, they will find a fair handful of passengers, mainly youngsters, leaving the train here to walk down to the beach and sea-front half a mile away. Seaton Carew is now mainly a residential suburb of Hartlepool, but some high-class hotels, residential as well as catering, still maintain their proud position on the promenade.

The train continues through a mixture of sidings, light industrial premises, and a rejuvenated housing estate. When it slows for a left-hand curve, just before Stranton signal box on the right, the traveller has time to enjoy the attractive view of Hartlepool Bay that gradually opens up. The well built-up peninsula that forms it is known as the Headland. Prominent among its landmarks is the abbey church of St Hilda, Saxon in origin, with a long and detailed history.

This view disappears once we curve past the docks and timber-storage wharves that herald our approach to the curved platform of Hartlepool (formerly West Hartlepool) station. Four colourful murals on the opposite wall of the station portray in collage form some of the town's more scenic views, traditional industries and sports facilities.

HARTLEPOOL

The name 'Hartlepool' has for so long been synonymous with music-hall jokes that visitors may be surprised to find how much of genuine worth there is to see in this town of 91,000 people. Leaving the station and turning left down Church Street and over the level-crossing, the visitor will reach the site of (and gain an increasing idea of the future appearance of) Hartlepool's Marina. This is an ambitious project in which Teesside's Development Corporation hopes to rejuvenate the Old Town district and the dock area with up-market housing and leisure facilities. Retracing steps northwards, past Church Square, a bus station and the Central Library (due for resiting some distance away before long), the visitor comes to Clarence Road, a right turning. Past the *Mail* newspaper offices is the Gray Art Gallery and Museum, a Victorian mansion-like structure. This, as well as being worthy of a visit in its own right, happens to be close to the best bus-stop for services (nos. 3 or 7, Hartlepool Transport or 'Tees' buses) every few minutes to the Headland, St Hilda's church, the Old Town Walls and an excavation site. The buses are marked 'Middlegate' in all cases.

Further from the centre, starting about ten minutes' walk away from the station along the Stockton Road, will be found the Burn Valley Gardens. These start very unpretentiously as little more than surroundings to a children's play area, but broaden out into a series of linked formal garden areas, leading past the Burn Valley bowling-green to the open country at the western edge of the town, about a mile in all. Various walks beyond this point are possible, through the countryside towards Elwick or Dalton Piercy villages, but it is best to check beforehand at the Tourist Information Bureau, which is tucked inside the large modern red-brick Civic Centre in Victoria Road, in central Hartlepool.

The remarkably undulating journey to Elwick may also be made by bicycle or by bus. A former Director of Education for Hartlepool, faced with job applicants who were in two minds about moving to Hartlepool from elsewhere, sometimes gave them a run out into the countryside along this road to Elwick, and claimed it never failed to persuade them in Hartlepool's favour! For those who wish to test this theory for themselves, the hourly no. 236 bus route operated by TMS (Trimdon Motor Services) to Sedgefield dovetails very neatly at present with daytime train arrivals at Hartlepool from both Middlesbrough and Newcastle (provided these are punctual!), and the journey time to Elwick from the town bus-station is about twenty minutes. Sadly connections from Elwick by bus to the Middlesbrough trains at Hartlepool are usually poor.

Those who break their rail journey at Hartlepool, for these or any other touring purposes, should be warned that, for most of the day, only one of the two through-platforms is used by passenger trains. This means that whether you are going north or south, the train will leave from platform 2. If you rush on to Hartlepool station at the last minute for your train, and see a diesel unit standing in the platform, do check that it is actually going the way you want and not another train running late and going elsewhere. Even daily regulars have to do this from time to time!

HARTLEPOOL–SUNDERLAND

Leaving Hartlepool, past docks and timber-yards, the train climbs steadily to the point where the line to 'Old' Hartlepool (on the Headland) once formed a triangular junction. The Steetley Magnesite factory is passed on the right. BR handles much train-load traffic between here and Thrislington, usually via the Norton–Ferryhill goods link (see page 26) and is likely to do so for many years to come.

Next, and possibly to many passengers' surprise, the train reaches a considerable stretch of scenic coast, with the golf course on the seaward side flanking Hart and its growing village area inland. Hart station was closed in 1953 (a footbridge marks the spot), and Cleveland County Council wants to reinstate it now that the area has grown into a desirable suburb of Hartlepool.

Our route is soon passing a large but neatly laid-out caravan park at Crimdon, whose dene (a narrow valley with a stream running along it) is a local beauty spot, and the coastal outlook remains rural and peaceful. There is even a sandy beach. The sea, often crashing over it in large breakers, is clearly visible from the train on those days when sea mist is not about. Even the village of Blackhall to the left, where there was formerly a busy colliery, does not interrupt the rural dream, though it must be said that soon afterwards the pit villages on the landward side of the track most certainly do. Before then, however, the line runs in cutting for quite a way, and emerges suddenly on a high stone viaduct across the spectacular Castle Eden Dene, which, anywhere else, would have gained more fame and publicity than the hinterlands of Horden, the next village we pass, and Easington Colliery, a couple of miles further on. Easington, Horden, and Blackhall each had a station until the late 1950s, but plans to reopen Horden, which go back several years, are meeting with less success than had been hoped. Horden is the nearest point on the railway to Peterlee new town, a mile or two inland.

Quite successful efforts have been made to reclaim and landscape the areas north of Hartlepool, previously occupied by working coal-mines. Indeed, anyone revisiting the Durham Coast Line after more than a twenty-year absence will be astonished at how little impact the coal industry now makes on the scenery. Coal trains, however, run in plenty. One source is the mine and sidings at Dawdon where, a few minutes after the train has curved to the right past Easington Colliery and signal box, urban industry puts paid to seaside idylls for the short stretch to Seaham station. Before the train slows down, passengers may catch a view of Seaham harbour some distance away on the right. Then the National Coal Board's branch crosses beneath us a bit further on, immediately preceding the unusual level-crossing – no road vehicles are allowed through it, only pedestrians – at the south end of Seaham station.

After Seaham the train should travel comparatively slowly into a small wood past Hall Dene signal box, then through a gentle 'S'-shaped double curve to regain a brief contact with the coast and occasional tantalising views of sandy and pebbled beaches. Then, on the left, is the site of Ryhope Junction station, another instance where a footbridge is the only surviving indication. It straddles not our line, but the former branch to South Hetton and Shotton Collieries. In Ryhope itself is a Victorian pumping station which is open to the public, and in steam on Bank Holiday weekends.

After one last short rural interlude, the urban areas take over as the borough of Sunderland is traversed at fair speed, with lengthy tunnels giving fair warning of the approach of Sunderland station. The almost totally subterranean nature of this station prevents the traveller from realising on a first visit how neatly it is laid out, how spacious its premises are above platform level, and how remarkably central it is to the main shopping streets of Wearside's largest town with a population of 217,000.

Within a few minutes of the station you can reach the Empire Theatre, the Crowtree Leisure Centre with its large indoor swimming-pool, and, under the protective shadow of the modern Civic Centre, Mowbray Park, with its lake overlooked by the public library.

SUNDERLAND–NEWCASTLE

Those who stay on, or rejoin, the train at Sunderland pass through another short tunnel and then cross the River Wear on a short viaduct. A brief glimpse may be caught of Sunderland's shipyards, or much closer, of Wearmouth road bridge's massive curved arch to the right. If this structure reminds the passenger of either Sydney Harbour Bridge or the Tyne Bridge in Newcastle, this is exactly as intended. Do not savour the resemblance too long though, or you will miss the ensuing period-piece of Monkwearmouth station, a listed building now containing a railway museum that is open daily throughout the year. Some of its exhibits remain outside, on the right, in full view of rail travellers. Sadly, the train no longer stops at this station but there is a case for reopening it now that the museum is well established.

Soon we reach Seaburn, a station opened in 1937, also serving the seaside suburb of Roker, three quarters of a mile away. By leaving the railway temporarily at Seaburn and going back on oneself towards Sunderland, it is possible to combine a visit to Monkwearmouth station museum with a walk along England's north-east coast for a mile or two on the promenade. For much of each autumn, this boasts illuminations of some considerable variety, though not on the scale of those in Blackpool. Meanwhile, apart from a brief interlude each side of the pleasant rural community of East Boldon, the line threads through a virtually continuous built-up area. Clattering across a flat rail-crossing (Pontop), we curve through the staggered platforms of Boldon Colliery station, actually nearer to Hedworth. Then, a few minutes after crossing the A1 on its route to the Tyne Road Tunnel, we meet the South Shields Metro line as it passes over our heads from right to left before descending to join our route at Pelaw. The original main line from Ferryhill and Leamside, still used for diversions, joins us on our left. Before long our train pulls up at Heworth Interchange.

Those who resist the temptation to transfer to the laudably frequent Metro trains will now find that the two routes parallel each other until just after Gateshead Stadium Metro station, when ours veers to the right through a goods yard. Our train slows down in sight of Newcastle's many monuments and landmarks, such as the Byker Wall housing development cross the river, and takes a sharp 'S'-bend past the site of the former Gateshead East station, closed in 1981 on the opening of the Metro system, and on to High Level Bridge. This is a combined road and rail structure whose upper deck has recently had a weight-limit imposed on it. The Tyne crossing, immediately in front of the Castle Keep, brings the train to Newcastle Central station.

TYNE VALLEY LINE
by John Bourn

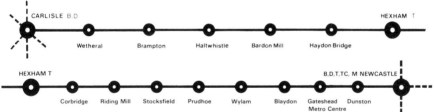

Background

The Tyne Valley Line was the culmination of a series of attempts to link Newcastle and Carlisle by use of the Tyne Gap, a structural pass between the uplands of the North Pennines and Southern Cheviots.

After an abortive attempt to build a canal, a railway, costing an estimated £252,488 was proposed, and the newly-formed Newcastle & Carlisle Railway Company began construction of the line in 1830. The first section, between Blaydon and Hexham, opened in March 1835.

Opening of the Hexham to Carlisle stage of the line, on 18 June 1838, should have been a day of triumph, but matters started to go wrong from the very beginning. When several dignitaries, attempting to board a steam packet at Redheugh on the River Tyne, crowded too hastily onto a gangplank, it promptly collapsed, giving them an unexpected immersion in the Tyne's murky waters! After drying out, they arrived late at the station to discover their seats already taken, and many of the railway's directors (as well as the Mayor of Newcastle) and their wives had to settle for plank seats in an open car. Departure from Carlisle on the return journey was in the midst of a thunderstorm, resulting in their second soaking of the day! A train collision at Milton then derailed the train, resulting in a lengthy wait for rescue in the pouring rain. Arrival back on Tyneside was in the early hours of the next morning, but only after another collision *en route*! If such a sorry tale of woe were to befall the railways today, some commentators would no doubt claim that it indicated the need for railway privatisation.

Thankfully, matters went more smoothly thereafter, and completion of the last stretch, into Newcastle, was in 1839. Britain's first cross-country railway was in operation. Since then, various branch lines have come and gone, but the Tyne Valley Line survives intact – albeit not without inevitable rationalisation in recent years.

Retrenchment – and a brighter future?

The late 1950s saw the introduction of diesel multiple units (DMUs) to the line to cut costs, but that did not prevent Dr Beeching proposing in 1962 that virtually all the line's intermediate stations would be closed. The line itself would survive, and indeed would be needed to carry passengers between Newcastle and Scotland, since the Beeching Plan envisaged closure of the East Coast Main Line north of Newcastle.

Thankfully, neither idea went ahead, although some of the quieter stations were closed, and 1967 was to see Elswick, Fourstones, Gilsland, Greenhead, Head's Nook and Wetheral stations lose their train services. Wetheral station was later reopened, while Gilsland and Greenhead have been suggested from time to time as candidates for reopening. Although neither community is large, a station at either would plug a gap in the longest stretch of the line without a station (between Haltwhistle and Brampton), and would give ramblers and sightseers closer access to Hadrian's Wall.

The same year saw Paytrains introduced to the line, but it was to be another nineteen years before the ubiquitous DMUs were largely replaced by Class 143 Pacer railbuses, whose catalogue of defects since then have exercised the minds of frustrated passengers and BR managers alike! By then, trains were running between Newcastle and Blaydon along the south bank of the Tyne, having been re-routed along the former freight line in 1983, to avoid expensive track renewals on the existing line. The new routeing has enabled stations to be opened at Dunston (replacing one closed in 1926) and Gateshead Metro Centre. The other 'new' station on the line is Wetheral, reopened in 1981.

To bring the story right up to date, Class 156 Super Sprinter trains were introduced in October 1988, to run new through-services between Newcastle and south-west Scotland, generating a 36% increase in revenue along the route of the new service. With station modernisation and installation of public address equipment in hand, the Tyne Valley Line continues to prosper as it enters the 1990s.

The Journey – Newcastle to Hexham

To reach the start of the Tyne Valley Line proper, trains need to cross the Tyne by either one of Newcastle's two railway bridges: the High Level to the east of the station, or the King Edward to the west. Accordingly, you may have the unusual experience of catching your westbound train from a platform on the east side of the station! Whichever bridge you cross, the train will eventually descend beneath the level of the adjacent East Coast Main Line in a deep cutting before tunnelling below it and emerging on a downhill gradient amid Gateshead's suburban housing. It is hardly a scenic vista, but ahead, trees and gardens spring out of their shabby surroundings. The riot of greenery testifies that the area to the right of the line is the site of the 1990 Gateshead Garden Festival, which has its own miniature railway. For the duration of the Festival, ring 091-487 0722 for details.

Dunston is the first permanent station we reach (some trains do not stop here). You may wish to close your eyes at the industrial dereliction surrounding the line past Dunston, but visitors to the region should keep their eyes open long enough to observe the pigeon lofts typical of the North East which can be seen on the bankside to your right just past the station.

To exemplify the fact that the North East can be a place of contrasts, the landscape of run-down industry on the banks of the Tyne past Dunston transforms abruptly into the gleaming steel and glass of the Metro Centre. About sixty trains a day stop at the station here, opened in 1987, and your train may empty suddenly at this point. Some through-trains from Sunderland terminate here.

The statistics of the Metro Centre are staggering. It took 20,000 people to build it at a cost of £3.7 million per month. It employs over 5,500 people, attracted 20 million visitors in 1989 (including coach parties from as far afield as Northern Ireland, Norfolk and Devon), and comprises 360 shops, a 28-lane bowling alley and a 10-screen cinema. Books of discount vouchers are often available to passengers travelling by rail to the Metro Centre; enquire at Newcastle station.

Past the Metro Centre, dereliction is again widespread, although even here, efforts are being made to brighten things up: note the marina to your right. We are running along the north bank of the Tyne now, and the train rattles over a level-crossing before running into Blaydon station, which was obviously once on a much grander scale. The substantial station buildings which used to stand here had become an eyesore by the 1970s, and were demolished in 1978. Also gone is Blaydon Racecourse, immortalised in the famous Geordie song.

Once past Blaydon, the line becomes more rural in character. Industry gives way to woodland and meadow as we approach Wylam, where the original 1835 Station Master's house survives. Note also the fine signal box spanning the line here. This is one of two NER overhead gantry signal boxes on the line, the other being at Hexham.

Past Wylam station, the train runs along an embankment above the Tyne, with views of the village across the river. As the line bears right, you will see a distinctive bridge spanning the river, like a miniature version of Newcastle's famous Tyne Bridge. This originally carried a duplicate line between Wylam and Scotswood, which closed in 1968. The trackbed was converted into a riverside footpath during the 1970s, and makes for pleasant, gentle walking, with plenty of blackberries in season. Follow the path to the east and, about a quarter of a mile from the village, you come to Stephenson's Cottage, where the railway pioneer was born in 1781. Now owned by the National Trust, the cottage is open from Easter till October each year, on Wednesday, Saturday and Sunday, between 1.00 and 5.30 p.m. Wylam's Falcon Centre houses a Railway Museum, open on Tuesdays and Thursdays between 2.00 and 5.00 p.m. and 5.30 to 7.30 p.m. It is also open on Saturday mornings. For details, ring Wylam 3520.

Beyond Wylam, the line passes Kimberley-Clark's factory on the left as it approaches Prudhoe station, dominated by the castle standing on the hill to the left. Owned by English Heritage, part of it is open to the public. The town of Prudhoe is further up the hill. It is a stiff climb, and visitors may prefer to cross the bridge over the river to the village of Ovingham. Thomas Bewick, the famous wood engraver, is buried in the village church.

Just behind Ovingham church, a stone stile marks the beginning of a path leading into the attractive Whittle Dene, starting point for a series of pleasant walks described in local guidebooks. The dene is associated with the legend of 'Long Lonkin', a notorious freebooter, whose name is closely linked with nearby Nafferton Tower, the remains of which can be seen to the left of the dene, just north of the A69 road. A little further north, the Whittle Burn enters a rock pool known as Whirl Dub, by a small waterfall. Here, Lonkin is reputed to have flung his booty into the pool to evade capture, after committing robbery and murder at Welton Hall further upstream. Lady Welton's ghost is said to haunt the hall. All these places are accessible by public footpath, adding interest to a lovely walk, although it is hard to associate this peaceful countryside with such violent events.

Returning to the railway, the line, still hugging the south bank of the river, now reaches the village of Stocksfield. This was one of a number of stations refurbished

Pacer diesel train calls at Wetheral on a Carlisle–Newcastle service (*Photo:* Tom Heavyside)

by BR in 1989 with new signing and new waiting shelters. In the case of Stocksfield, existing stone waiting shelters were cleaned up. Again, Stocksfield is the starting-point for a number of attractive walks. To the south, quiet roads and tracks can take you to Broomley, a small village on the windswept ridge overlooking the Tyne Valley, where the views are splendid and the sense of isolation profound. For a gentler walk, exit from the eastbound platform of the station, and follow the road to Bywell Bridge spanning the Tyne, built in 1838. This is a popular spot, where you can often buy an ice-cream on summer weekends. Just past the bridge, there is a public footpath sign on your left. The path leads you through a small paddock, and emerges close to the fifteenth-century Bywell Castle. Turn left for Bywell village, a seductive hamlet on the banks of the Tyne, with a lovely sense of peace and serenity, especially in the sun-dappled churchyard at the end of the road overlooking the river.

By now, industry is well behind us, and the line has fully assumed its true rural character. More peaceful countryside follows before we arrive at our next stop, Riding Mill, serving a prosperous commuter village. The Wellington pub, at the end of the station approach road, does an excellent, good-value meal in pleasant surroundings.

Next stop is Corbridge, serving an attractive small town about half a mile from the station, across the river. It has grown considerably in recent years, thanks to an influx of Tyneside-based commuters, but it still retains its rural character. Corstopitum Roman Fort lies just west of the town, in the care of English Heritage. There are numerous eating places in Corbridge, and indeed the railway station house itself has been converted into a French restaurant.

We run through wide, spacious fields and a belt of woodland, before the first sight of industry for some time, indicating that we are approaching Hexham, the main town of the Tyne Valley, where many of the local trains terminate. The station has changed little from Victorian times and remains a beautifully-preserved local station, kept spotlessly clean by its dedicated staff. It even retains a busy freight yard, conveying timber and resins to the nearby Egger wood-products factory. Ballast for the north-ern area of BR's Eastern Region is also stored here, and loaded daily onto civil engineers' trains.

The town of Hexham
Set on a hill, and crowned by its splendid abbey, Hexham is a lovely stone-built market town. The abbey dates from AD 674, and the local Tourist Information Centre is housed in the thirteenth-century Manor Office and Moot Hall. There is also a cinema, arts centre and library, Border history museum and a riverside country park, plus a wide variety of shops and eating places, and a Tuesday market. For full details, ring the TIC on (0434) 605225. One piece of information which may be of intererst: Mrs Miggins' Coffee House, near the library and arts centre, was named after the coffee house frequently referred to by Rowan Atkinson's character in the *Black Adder* TV series. Rowan Atkinson, 'Mr B' himself, whose family live in Tynedale, has visited the shop to wish it well.

The Journey continued – Hexham to Haltwhistle
The route out of Hexham is less than idyllic, passing a scrapyard and an industrial estate before rural normality returns. We pass through the villages of Warden and Fourstones, and the line bears left, the valley opening out to give a panoramic view from the train window. And then suddenly, to emphasise again that this is a line of contrasts, trees close in and we run through a gorge-like stretch with the Tyne close by on our left, white water running over the boulder-strewn channel. Equally abruptly, the valley opens out again, and the village of Haydon Bridge can be seen ahead.

This is another station smartened up during 1989, with a new shelter provided on the westbound platform. Note the attractive arched entrance bearing the station name. There are pubs and shops in the village, plus a restaurant and a couple of small cafés. The village church is built partly with stones from an older Anglo-Saxon church which once stood near here, and which briefly housed St Cuthbert's remains in the ninth century.

For keen walkers, Haydon Bridge is the starting point for a fine 8-mile walk to Bardon Mill, described in the book *20 Great Walks from British Rail* (Sigma Press).

After Haydon Bridge, we cross three bridges: over the River South Tyne, the River Allen, and the South Tyne again. Beyond Hexham, the Tyne in fact divides into the North Tyne and the South Tyne.

The next station, Bardon Mill, largely rebuilt by BR in 1984, serves a tiny village. There is not much here but a pub, a post office and the Errington Reay pottery works. The original mill is long gone. Vindolanda Roman fort is a couple of miles uphill from Bardon Mill. Hadrian's Wall itself, and Housesteads Roman museum and fort are further north again. Unless you're a keen walker, the connecting bus which runs during the summer from Hexham station is the best way of getting to Housesteads and the various other museums and information centres on the wall. Both House-steads and Vindolanda are open all year. Visit them on a grey wintry day, with a cold wind blowing from the north, and you will be able to identify with the feelings of the hapless Roman centurions. Beautiful *and* bleak describes the countryside around here.

South of Bardon Mill, in a more sheltered, wooded environment, is Allen Banks Estate, 194 acres of wood and parkland gifted to the nation by Frances Bowes Lyon, a relative of the Queen Mother, in 1942. At its heart is the River Allen, running through a deep gorge, with numerous seats and picnic spots and tempting woodland walks. The hamlet of Beltingham, between Bardon Mill and Allen Banks, is one of the most seductive in Northumberland. A 900-year-old yew tree stands in the peaceful church-yard on a slight hill above the valley.

With the river still on our left and the scenery becoming gradually wilder, it's a short run to Haltwhistle, our next stop. As we approach the town, note the new siding on the left, evidence of new freight development. Plenmeller Common, to the south, is being developed as an open-cast coal-mine and, from 1991, coal will be carried by overhead conveyor to the siding, for onward transport by rail.

The approach to Haltwhistle is dominated by the Crown Paints factory to the left and beyond that the viaduct which once carried the Alston branch line over the river. Haltwhistle is a small town with a thirteenth-century church and a traffic problem. Department of Transport proposals for a relief road would effectively cut the railway station off from the town, but the proposed road has had a cool reception from townspeople and local MPs and may not go head. The station is well-kept and retains much of its historical character. Note the imposing signal box and the locomotive water columns which have outlived the end of steam operation. The goods yard still sees occasional use for the shipment of the 'Kilfrost' de-icing solution used by BR, which is made here.

The Alston Branch

The scenic branch line to Alston in Cumbria, England's highest market town, was opened in 1852, with four intermediate stations and spectacular viaducts at Halt-whistle and Lambley, which still exist. As it was built mainly to service the lead mines around Alston, the passenger service was always meagre, ranging from four to eight trains each way per day. Because roads to Alston were often blocked by snow in winter months, the railway acted as a life-line, and for this reason the Minister of Transport refused consent to its closure in 1963. A further closure application succeeded in 1973, conditional upon provision of an adequate road to carry a replacement bus service.

It has been argued that the line was closed in order to justify the building of an expensive new road to serve a small town of just 2,000 people. The cost of the new road, approximately £750,000, was about ten times the annual loss of the railway line, plus £2,000 per year for snow clearance and a £5,000 annual subsidy for the replacement bus service. Despite the cost of snow clearance (which would be given a high priority, objectors to the closure were told) during the winter of 1978–79, the replacement bus service was completely cancelled on six separate days and disrupted on another ten. Not surprisingly, only 23% of former rail passengers were still using the replacement bus service in 1980.

An excellent visual record of the Alston branch just before closure can be found on the *Video Track 13* railway video tape (Transport Video Publishing). It underlines that, had the line survived a few more years, it would have been subject to the more enlightened attitude of BR's current Provincial management, and would no doubt have been heavily promoted for its tourist potential, like many current branch lines. Sadly, it was not to be. The Alston branch line was one of the last rural branch lines to be closed in this country.

The South Tynedale Railway Preservation Society

Founded in 1973 with the original intention of running standard-gauge trains over the whole length of the branch, the Society was forced to scale down its aims, and it now runs a narrow-gauge service to a temporary terminus at Gilderdale Halt, the eventual intention being to run to Slaggyford, 5 miles from Alston.

The existing journey is a short but pleasant one, with the River South Tyne close by on our right, and hills on the left sweeping up to the main Brampton road and the moorland beyond. The route beyond the present terminus includes some of the finest views on the line, as well as a number of major bridges, and one can only wish the Society well in their endeavours to penetrate further down the valley.

Alston station has been beautifully restored by Cumbria County Council, incorporating a bookshop, toilets and tea-rooms, and the land between railway and river has been landscaped to provide a car park and picnic area.

Both the railway and Alston itself are well worth visiting, and while no substitute for the train, the bus journey from Haltwhistle (service 681) is most scenic. During summer Sundays in 1989, a bus service ran from Alston over the fells into Weardale, connecting there with the special train service operating from Stanhope to Darlington. By also making use of the Alston–Haltwhistle bus service, and the existing rail services from Haltwhistle to Newcastle, and Newcastle to Darlington, a spectacular bus and rail round-trip became possible, giving access to a wild upland area with normally very limited public transport links. At the time of writing, it seems likely that a similar service will continue to operate in future years, but it would be advisable to check first with Durham County Council, who sponsored the service (see Further Information section at end of book).

Final stage – Haltwhistle to Carlisle
The train leaves Haltwhistle in a deep cutting, giving few glimpses of the town, before running parallel to the A69 trunk road for around 3 miles, parting company at Greenhead. The Carvoran Roman fort is near here and the railway crosses the line of Hadrian's Wall, although little can be seen. Note the ruins of Thirlwall Castle, on a hill to the right.

The railway bears left and runs high above the village of Gilsland, straddling the Northumberland/Cumbria border. Here there are the remains of a Roman mile-castle and a rare glimpse of Hadrian's Wall. There now follows the most attractive section of the line, the railway running high above the valley of the River Irthing, with splendid views to the north, towards the Scottish borders.

This is deserted, peaceful countryside, which may look green and inviting or forbiddingly bleak, depending on when you see it. Lanercost Priory lies to the north, just across the river; to the south is a much starker landscape of hill and moorland, where few cars disturb the silence of the lonely country roads. There is a lake, Tindale Tarn, hidden away from view in a fold of the hills and a couple of small upland villages, but otherwise nothing to disturb the birds or the ghosts of the miners who once dug for lead in these windswept fells.

Public transport links are scarce in this area, but walkers will be grateful for our next stop, Brampton station, standing in splendid isolation next to a saw-mill and little else. Once you changed here for the branch line to Brampton Town, a short-lived enterprise which closed in the 1920s. The trackbed curving away into the woods beside the eastbound platform is now a public footpath, and forms a pleasanter (and safer) route to the town than the busy road at the end of the station approach.

The town of Brampton is largely undistinguished, and, standing at the convergence of a number of busy roads, suffers badly from traffic noise and vibration. But it does have shops and restaurants, which are scarce in this quiet area.

One place definitely worth visiting is Talkin Tarn, a popular local beauty spot, which is fortunately easily-reached from the station. Go out of the gate on the westbound platform on to the country lane and turn right. Follow the road for about three quarters of a mile as it begins to climb slightly uphill. Close to the crest of the hill on your left is a gate leading into a field. Follow the clear track through the field for about half a mile, aiming for the belt of trees up ahead. A gate gives access into this small wood surrounding the tarn, and any number of paths will lead you to the tarn itself. Surrounded by hills, this is a lovely spot, and in summer you can buy ice-cream, sweets and hot drinks. There are also maps of the area and details of its wildlife. A path leads around the tarn to the Talkin Hotel, in case you feel like something more substantial in the way of refreshments. The road beyond the hotel leads into Talkin village, where there are pubs and a shop, and continues past the village into the lonely hills above.

Rejoining the train, we pass Brampton Golf Course, and then descend in a cutting towards the Eden Valley, crossing on a spectacular viaduct into Wetheral station. The original buildings still survive, giving the station a true 'country railway' atmosphere. Wetheral is a prosperous-looking village, with a ruined priory and riverside walks. Walk far enough and you can reach Armathwaite, on the Settle–Carlisle line.

But the suburbs of Carlisle now approach us. Here you can travel by electric train to Glasgow or north-west England; cross the Pennines again via the Settle–Carlisle line; ride down the Cumbrian Coast to Barrow; or explore south-west Scotland. Or, if you've had enough travelling, Carlisle itself has much to offer: castle, cathedral, riverside paths, the Lanes shopping centre and more. Whatever your destination, enjoy your day – and remember, you don't have to look for a parking space!

TYNESIDE AND GALLOWAY SPRINTERS
by Graham Lund

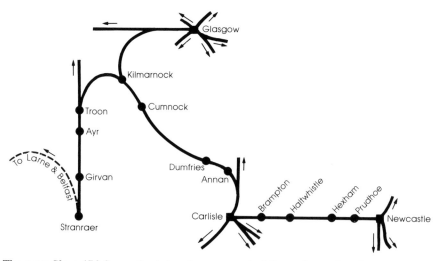

The new Class 156 Super Sprinters have operated through-services between Newcastle and south-west Scotland since October 1988, joining up two once distinct routes and adding another. The loss of the daytime Stranraer–Euston services were partially compensated by a Stranraer–Newcastle through-train. Current daily services from Newcastle are two trains to Glasgow, two to Dumfries, and one each to Stranraer and Girvan. In the reverse direction there are two daily trains from Glasgow and one each from Girvan and Stranraer to Newcastle.

These trains show signs of tapping the lead sales potential of the routes they serve. They connect heavily populated Tyneside, running via Gateshead and its Metro Centre, to Carlisle for connections for much of the country. From there, through-trains run to Dumfries with its bustling shopping centre and buses for the Galloway towns.

From Dumfries, northbound trains head up the beautiful Nith Valley route with its mixture of rich agricultural land and wooded hillside. At Kirkconnel we note the transition into the mining zone with its open-cast sites near the station. The line then joins the Afton Water and follows its course up the valley to New Cumnock, where the station reopened in the spring of 1990. A further call is made at Auchinleck before we proceed into 'Burns Country'.

Kilmarnock is the home of Robert Burns' first edition and the monument to the bard is visible from the station. The town is also host to the largest whisky-bottling plant in the world, situated next to the station, which forms part of a busy railway junction. Here the lines diverge.

Trains bound for Glasgow continue up the ex-Glasgow, Barrhead, and Kilmarnock joint line through the villages of Kilmaurs, Stewarton and Dunlop over a steeply-graded line which then descends to Barrhead and Glasgow. Trains for the coastal stations run down the branch line through agricultural and industrial land towards Barassie Junction. Immediately north is the large paper mill, now in operation and served by rail. Here our Sprinter joins the electrified line from Glasgow to Ayr.

Troon is our next stop and is the occasional home to the British Open Golf Championship. We then pass Prestwick Airport and into Ayr station. This thriving town is a busy tourist and agricultural centre and is home to the Scottish Grand National and large agricultural and horticultural shows. Burns was born in Alloway where his first home still stands. He praised his home town for its 'honest men and bonnie lasses'.

Southbound, we call at Maybole, which serves as railhead for the bus link to Turnberry when the British Open 'calls' here. Next stop is Girvan which sees the start of the Carrick Hills. The town has a small fishing fleet and distillery. Offshore is Paddy's Milestone, local name for Ailsa Craig, home to a major gannet colony.

Further south we call at Barrhill on a tortuous, hilly stretch of track before the descent into the port of Stranraer, where we can connect for the ferry for Larne.

TANFIELD RAILWAY
by David Hagerty

The Tanfield Railway lies in the hills of North Durham, some 6 miles south-west of Gateshead, close to the village of Sunniside.

For non-motorists, Sunniside can be reached by bus from Gateshead or Newcastle, service X11, X30, 705-8 on weekdays (706, 708 on Sundays), and X75 Tourist bus stops by Marley Hill shed on summer Sundays. You can cycle from Newcastle, Blaydon or the nearest station, Dunston. Indeed, part of the former trackbed of the Tanfield Railway is now a cycleway, starting at a roundabout south of Dunston station and leading up to Sunniside.

The main site is off the Sunniside–Stanley road. On approaching it there appears to be nothing of note, just a landscape showing the barely-healed scars of nineteenth-century mining activity. But walk across the car park at the site entrance and ahead, in a hollow, is a scene which belongs firmly in the industrial past of County Durham.

For this is nothing if not an industrial railway. A small band of enthusiasts has succeeded in re-creating an authentic atmosphere which is rarely found in places conceived as tourist attractions. The purpose is to create a colliery railway from the days of steam, where public passenger trains performed a valuable service but were clearly a secondary function.

The Tanfield Railway, began as a four-foot gauge wooden railway in 1725, was rebuilt as a standard-gauge line in 1839 and operated as part of the North Eastern Railway. Ironically for a preserved industrial railway it has a place in railway history as the first passenger-carrying branch line in the world, in 1842. Passengers were carried in rudimentary rolling stock, and the service was soon withdrawn for lack of support.

After more than a century carrying freight, the line closed in stages between 1947 and 1981, but since 1973 the Tanfield Railway Society has also been operating. Passenger services, to a better standard of comfort than 150 years ago, now run from the main site with platforms in Marley Hill yard and at nearby Andrew's House, to Sunniside. Trains run every Sunday, some weekdays in midsummer and on Bank Holiday

Mondays, with 'Santa Specials' in December. Marley Hill engine-shed is open daily as well, for viewing.

This engine-shed, built in 1955 and now the oldest in Britain still in its original use, is the centre-piece of the railway. The shed and its yard are crowded with industrial locomotives, and look much as they must have done in the early years of this century. The atmosphere is enhanced by demonstration freight trains. The growing collection of carriages is based on nineteenth-century non-bogie stock.

Track has been relaid from Andrew's House platform to Causey Arch, and it is hoped a service will start by the end of 1990. Track will ultimately be relaid to East Tanfield. The arch, which spans a deep, wooded gorge, dates from 1725 and is the world's oldest railway bridge. Its surroundings have been made into a picnic area, and a viewing platform constructed overlooking the arch. The more energetic, with time on their hands, may contemplate a walk of a further 2½ miles to the Beamish Museum.

BEAMISH MUSEUM
by Geoffrey Longstaff

Beamish is England's first regional open-air museum. Created in 1970 to preserve the heritage of the north-east of England, it has grown steadily on its 200-acre site of woodland and rolling countryside. There are many exhibits, including 'The Town', 'Home Farm' and 'The Colliery', and further improvements are planned.

The transport collection includes the museum's electric tramcars, which provide a regular service around the site.

One of the highlights of the museums is the railway which is based around a typical country station of about 1910. The station was actually transported from the village of Rowley, near Consett, and includes a furnished Ladies' Waiting Room and a booking office. Nearby a signal box can be visited, again originally from the Consett area, while the wrought-iron footbridge started life at Howden-le-Wear.

Goods and coal wagons are to be found in the adjoining goods yard along with various locomotives, including a working replica of *Locomotion*, the first engine built

Beamish Open Air Museum (*Photo:* Tom Heavyside)

for a public railway. These can best be seen in action on Steam Day in September, with the relatively short line routed round the back of the nearby 'Town' and terminating at 'The Pit Cottages'. A branch is also being developed from here to 'The Colliery'.

Beamish is open daily, except for Mondays during November–March (at the time of writing). Further information can be obtained from North of England Open Air Museum, Beamish Hall, Stanley, Co. Durham, tel. Stanley (0207) 231811.

An hourly bus service operates to Beamish from Durham (Millburngate, a few minutes from the railway station) and is run by J. Hammel (Diamond Coaches, service 720). Further information is available from them at Central Garage, Agnes Street, Stanley, Co. Durham, DH9 0DN, tel. 232430.

In July and August 1989, a popular package was offered by BR, a local coach operator and the museum, whereby people could book from any rail station in the country a ticket which included return rail fare to Durham, a coach connection to Beamish, and entry into the museum. It is hoped that such a package will again be offered in future years.

BOWES RAILWAY
by Trevor Garrod

Originating in 1826, the Bowes Railway on the southern outskirts of Gateshead was part of the Pontop & Jarrow Railway, over 15 miles long and serving up to thirteen collieries. It contained seven rope-worked inclines, with three sections that were sufficiently level to be worked by locomotives.

Pit closures led to the gradual closure of the lines serving them, and by 1974 only the Monkton–Jarrow section of this line was still in use. The section south of Gateshead was bought by the then Tyne and Wear County Council in 1976 and is now classified as an Ancient Monument, with 1¼ miles of track operated under a Light Railway Order since 1981. It includes the only preserved standard-gauge rope-worked incline in the world.

Attractions include the workshop complex, loco shed and trains running up to Blackham's Hill. These are normally open on summer Sundays and on Bank Holidays. For further information contact Bowes Railway Centre, Springwell Village, Gateshead, Tyne and Wear, NE9 7QJ, tel. 091-416 6956.

THE STEPHENSON RAILWAY MUSEUM
by David Hagerty

A collection of locomotives and rolling stock has been assembled at the Stephenson Railway Museum in Middle Engine Lane, North Shields. It includes George Stephenson's pioneering *Killingworth Billy*, one of the world's three oldest surviving locomotives. Also on display is *Silver Link*, a contemporary of the record-breaking *Mallard* and a regular performer on the East Coast Main Line during the 1930s.

A new steam railway has been built to link the museum with a platform close to Percy Main Metro station, a distance of 1½ miles. It is due to open in April 1990 and operate at weekends during the summer. Alternatively, Middle Lane is served by buses from Newcastle, North Shields, Whitley Bay and Cullercoats.

The museum is open daily, except Mondays, throughout the summer. For further details, telephone the museum on 091-262 2627.

Metro train leaves Kingston Park on a South Shields–Bank Foot service (*Photo:* John C. Baker)

TYNESIDE METRO
by John Bourn

The Tyneside Metro has dramatically modernised Tyneside's public transport system, reduced road congestion, and established itself as a model example of a cost-effective urban transport system, one studied keenly by planners from elsewhere in Britain and further afield.

The local lines to Whitley Bay, Tynemouth and South Shields, which formed the basis for the Metro, were electrified by the North Eastern Railway in 1904, but despite local opposition, were converted to diesel operation by British Rail in 1967. With shabby, ageing trains and often decrepit, vandalised stations, the local rail system was far from being a jewel in Tyneside's crown, and in the late 1960s, the newly-created Tyneside Passenger Transport Executive commissioned a study into the future of the local rail network, with options ranging from major reinvestment to conversion into express busways.

The most attractive solution was found to be a light rapid-transit system that would be cheaper and faster than traditional railway operation, and which would, by tunnelling, serve Newcastle city centre. A significant handicap for the existing rail network was that it terminated at Central Station, south of the city centre.

Ironically, Greater Manchester was also contemplating similar plans at this time, but Tyneside's transport chiefs were slightly quicker than their Manchester counterparts in submitting their plans to the government and so it was Tyneside which gained the money available, with Manchester having to wait another eighteen years to get its Metrolink scheme under way. Work began in 1974 on the city centre tunnels, and in 1978 the Tyne was spanned by the new Metro bridge. Just two years earlier, the scheme had nearly come to grief in the public spending cutbacks imposed by the then Labour government. 1980 saw the first section opened, from Haymarket to Tynemouth, with further sections following until final completion in 1984.

So was it worth it? An unequivocal 'yes' was given by the Department of Transport's own Transport and Road Research Laboratory in 1984, when it concluded that: 'Its benefits to public transport passengers, other road users and the community at large substantially exceed its operating costs . . .', which is more or less what the Tyneside public had already concluded for themselves! The cost of £280m may sound high, but as *Modern Railways* magazine said in 1982: '. . . at £5m per kilometre, inclusive of rolling stock, the system will still be one of the cheapest rapid-transit railways in the world.'

Metro operation

The system consists of four colour-coded lines. The yellow line runs from Pelaw into the centre of Newcastle, then loops round the coast to terminate back in the city at St James. The green line runs from Bank Foot to South Shields. These two lines make up the whole system, but there are also two duplicate routes: a red line from Pelaw to Benton via the city centre, and a blue line from North Shields to St James. All run at frequent intervals, giving a train every few minutes over the busiest section, from Pelaw to Benton. Trains normally consist of a pair of two-car units reduced to a single two-car unit on winter Sundays and in the evening. The trains are driver-only operated, with tickets sold by station ticket machines. Travel Centres at principal stations deal with queries and issue 'Traveltickets' for weekly, monthly or annual travel, plus 'Day Rover' tickets for visitors. A range of Metro merchandise is also sold. 'Explorer' tickets, valid on many bus services in the North East, are now accepted on the Metro also. There are Metro-bus interchange stations at Regent Centre, Four Lane Ends, North Shields, Wallsend, Byker, Gateshead, Heworth, Jarrow and Chichester, and there is interchange with the BR line to Sunderland and Middlesbrough at Central Station and Heworth.

The future

There were many fears that the 1985 Transport Act, allowing local bus services to compete freely with the Metro, could cripple the system and bring about the end of the Metro-bus through-ticketing then in use. Although this happened to a degree at first, the situation seems now to have stabilised with bus operators seemingly preferring to co-operate with the Metro, rather than engage in damaging competition. 1988 saw Metro-bus through-ticketing resume and the all-systems 'Traveltickets', allowing travel on local buses, Metro, Tyne ferry and Sunderland trains, continue to flourish.

Plans are now well underway to extend the Metro to Newcastle Airport. The next step being studied is a line from Heworth to Sunderland, via the new town of Washington, not presently served by a passenger railway, although this would be a much bigger and costlier project.

Lessons of the Metro

Since the Metro has been studied closely by other British cities wishing to develop their own rapid-transit systems, what lessons does it hold? Perhaps the main one is a cautionary one: that de-staffing can only be taken so far. The original plan was that station entrance barriers, allied to roving ticket inspectors, would prevent fraudulent travel, while violence or vandalism would be spotted by closed-circuit TV cameras and the police quickly called to the scene. In practice, the station barriers proved little deterrent to fare-dodgers, who simply vaulted over them, and most stations have now had these mechanisms removed. Similarly, by the time the police were called to apprehend vandals or troublemakers, the culprits had often fled. The Metro now has a much larger squad of revenue control inspectors, whose presence has had a gratifying effect on fare evasion, and it is soon to get its own complement of police to patrol the system. Proof, for those planning similar systems, that the human presence can be not only reassuring, but cost-effective also.

Metro ...

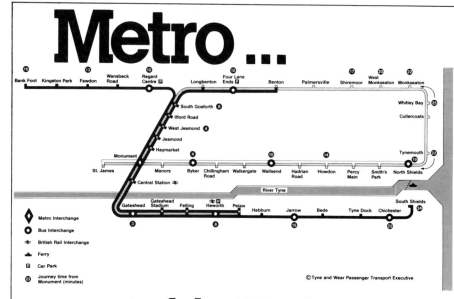

			Wansbeck	Regent		Four Lane					West	
Bank Foot	Kingston Park	Fawdon	Road	Centre	Longbenton	Ends	Benton	Palmersville	Shiremoor	Monkseaton	Monkseaton

South Gosforth
Ilford Road
West Jesmond
Jesmond
Haymarket
Monument
St. James
Central Station

Whitley Bay
Cullercoats
Tynemouth

Manors   Byker   Chillingham Road   Walkergate   Wallsend   Hadrian Road   Howdon   Percy Main   Smith's Park   North Shields

River Tyne

Gateshead   Gateshead Stadium   Felling   Heworth   Pelaw   Hebburn   Jarrow   Bede   Tyne Dock   Chichester   South Shields

- ◆ Metro Interchange
- ○ Bus Interchange
- ⇌ British Rail Interchange
- ⚓ Ferry
- P Car Park
- ㉒ Journey time from Monument (minutes)

©Tyne and Wear Passenger Transport Executive

...part of the North East's railway heritage

If George and Robert Stephenson were alive today, the chances are they would be commuting by Metro.

Our new Palmersville Station is just a short walk from their Killingworth home, where George was colliery engineer.

The North end of the Queen Elizabeth Bridge is on the site of their Forth Banks locomotive works, and from the bridge they could see Robert's High Level Bridge, the penultimate link in the East Coast Main Line, built in 1849.

Metro's railway heritage goes back more than 150 years. At South Shields, trains have been using these alignments since the Stanhope & Tyne line was built in 1834. Our oldest operational stations are at Tynemouth and Cullercoats, built for the North Eastern Railway in 1882.

You can follow in the Stephensons' footsteps and explore Tyneside's railway heritage with a Tyne and Wear Day Rover Ticket, available from Travel Centres.

For details of private metrotours and travel information, write to Tyne and Wear Metro, Cuthbert House, All Saints, Newcastle upon Tyne, NE1 2DA.

Metro *The only way to travel*

'YELLOW' METRO LINE
by Harold Atkinson

Newcastle and the Coast

The Metro map suggests that Pelaw or St James should be the starting point for describing the yellow line. Pelaw to the Central Station is described in the chapter dealing with the green line, therefore this chapter starts at Central Station.

Before descending to Metro Central Station to tour the yellow line, the visitor, especially if architecturally inclined, should inspect BR Central Station, undoubtedly one of the finest main-line buildings in the country. This station once ranked alongside the principal London termini for numbers of trains and passengers and, we hope, it may recover its former glory when the world's physical and resource limitations force a return to transport sanity. Some of it has been demolished to provide yet more city-centre car-parking. Surely, to be converted to a car park is the ultimate degradation for any station! Despite these amputations it remains an outstanding station. This is especially so externally, as the magnificent frontage and portico have been retained intact. A glimmer of hope for the future: two new platforms have been built as a consequence of the electrification of the East Coast Main Line.

There are three entrances to Metro Central, one of them in BR Central Station. The visitor should descend the escalator, go to the platform on the left at the bottom, and board a train marked 'St James'. This name will be displayed on a yellow background for easy visibility. Benton trains have their destination on a red background, and Bankfoot trains on a green background. The first station after Central is Monument. Despite the destination 'St James' anybody wanting to go to St James must change at Monument, otherwise he/she will add 20 miles to the journey and have to pay more. Monument is the busiest station on the Metro system and plays a major part in promoting city-centre shopping. Soon after this station opened, it was estimated that the number of shoppers in Eldon Square shopping centre had increased by about 30%. Haymarket is next: another busy station destined to become busier, as it is at the top of the recently pedestrianised Northumberland Street.

Jesmond is the third station and the Metro surfaces here to follow the former BR line to the coast. This line was electrified, third rail type, in 1904 and served the people on the north side of the Tyne faithfully and well until BR saw fit to de-electrify it in 1967.

Jesmond Dene, perhaps the only Newcastle park heard of outside the North East, is not as close as the station name suggests. The one-mile walk to it is pleasant enough in itself, but fast heavy traffic makes taking a bus a necessity. Jesmond Dene is an interesting and attractive semi-natural park, once the private grounds of Lord Armstrong, the multi-millionaire arms manufacturer and engineer. He presented it to the people of Newcastle and it now forms part of the extensive and unexpected system of parks possessed by the city. Those who knew Jesmond Dene before the Second World War will miss the red gravel paths which were such a striking feature. A trace of red can be spotted here and there by the keen-eyed. The park gives a good idea of what the other valleys in Newcastle must have looked like before they were filled in or built over as the city expanded.

West Jesmond station follows and is within easy walking-distance of the 'Town Moor'. The Town Moor would probably be called a 'common' in the south, but differs in being almost treeless. It is large indeed and contains Exhibition Park (formerly Bull Park) at its south-east corner on the rim of the city centre. It is suggested from time to time that the Town Moor be laid out as a park in the ordinary sense. Whatever the merit of these suggestions it is certainly a place where people can take a very long walk away from the traffic (except for crossing the Grandstand Road which bisects

47

it). The Freemen of Newcastle have an ancient right to graze cattle (but not bulls!) on the moor. Luckily, some still exercise this right: cattle are self-fuelling first-class lawn-mowers!

Ilford Road, the next station, was built specially for the Metro and is about half a mile from the northern end of Jesmond Dene (consult a street plan). South Gosforth is next and is the operations centre of the Metro system. Here the green route and the yellow route diverge, the green to head towards the north-west of Newcastle and the yellow to the coast.

There is little of interest between South Gosforth and the coast but this does not mean there is little of importance. Longbenton station was built soon after the war to provide easy travel to the DSS headquarters where about 10,000 people work. Were a direct footpath to be built, the station could also serve the large new Freeman Hospital. Four Lane Ends is next and was built specially as an interchange for the integrated transport system which was working so well until abolished by government order a few years ago. After this is Benton station, which retains much of its former LNER and BR appearance. Just beyond Benton the line passes over the East Coast Main Line and then over the route to Ashington. There are occasional rumours that the latter line will be restored to passenger use, but we are still waiting. A new station has been built at Palmersville and on leaving it the yellow line enters the green wedge. Do not be disheartened. This uninviting spur of the green belt is not typical of the North East. Why all building on it is prohibited is a mystery. The Metro makes it ideal for residential development.

Hammerhead crane on the lower Tyne (*Photo:* Harold Atkinson)

There is another new station at Shiremoor. It is busier than might have been predicted. West Monkseaton follows. This was built in the 1930s to cater for the expanding western part of Monkseaton. After this, the yellow line enters Monkseaton station, the first station suitable for visiting the coast. A walk of about half a mile to the sea-front is entailed but many people take it in their stride. The trackbed of the former Monkseaton to Blyth line can be seen immediately before entering the station. Those who like a pleasant, 'countrified' stroll would do well to alight at Monkseaton and walk along the trackbed which has been made into a walkway for about 3 miles, with the bonus of a wildlife pond close by near the end. Delaval Hall is a little further on but well worth taking a closer look at if time allows. Monkseaton is an attractive station and, apart from the ill-conceived demolition of the long glass canopy over the western-side platform, it is much as it was in LNER days.

Whitley Bay is the main station for the coast. It is an attractive station with an overall, though somewhat shortened, glass roof. It has lost, too, the external glass canopy which sheltered part of the very long queues which built up on summer weekend evenings, waiting to return home from a day at the seaside. The pro-road campaign which began in earnest in the 1950s drastically reduced the number of passengers, but it is heartening to see that, thanks to the Metro, passenger traffic is growing again. The sea-front is under five minutes' walk away.

Whitley Bay cannot be said to be a holiday resort in the same sense that many places on the south coast are, for there is no skyline of imposing hotels, not even one big hotel, but it has something which nevertheless acts as a magnet to visitors – the beach, with 'The Island' at the north end. St Mary's Island is a part-time island with a causeway making it accessible on foot for about two-thirds of the approximately twelve-hour tide cycle. It has a particularly striking and attractive lighthouse, abandoned by Trinity House, but saved from demolition by North Tyneside Council which bought it, helped by public subscription. The council is renovating it and converting the lighthouse and keeper's house into a visitors' centre. The public is already allowed to ascend the lighthouse much more frequently than when it was operational. The walk along the promenade and sands to 'The Island' should be a must in the visitor's schedule. The sand is fine and of a yellow-fawn tint. The downward shelving of the beach, though slight, is sufficient for the water's edge not to recede more than about a hundred yards at low tide.

The next coastal station is Cullercoats, not far from the beach. Until shortly after the war, Cullercoats was a picturesque working fishing village. The fish were caught locally in the characteristic cobles (semi-flat-bottomed boats). This ended a long time ago because, it is said, of the difficulties arising from new fish-marketing regulations. The village itself was planned out of existence except for a solitary row of cottages. The distinctly attractive bay with its two breakwaters remains unchanged, and is safe for swimming. The water is somewhat warmer than at the other beaches accessible by the yellow line, as it is more recessed. The North Sea is, however, rather cool. Cullercoats gained the European Blue Flag in 1989. As with all the beaches on the yellow route, the sand is fine, and ideal for 'plodging'. Plodging is the local expression for paddling – very apt for what it describes.

Tynemouth is the last of the coastal stations before the line turns back inland. It is an impressive example of the best of Victorian non-main-line stations. It was in major jeopardy but has been saved and is undergoing massive restoration. Two of its platforms are used by the Metro, but the others are not, however, being returned to railway use. Tynemouth beach, in the eyes of many, is the finest on the yellow line, although strangely, less popular than Whitley Bay. Rounding the rocks at the south end or, perhaps less hazardly, going up the slope or steps to the footpath, the visitor will see a second beach, King Edward's Bay. Again, this has high quality sand. The cliff headland is crowned with Tynemouth Priory and Castle. The whole headland is well laid-out and looked after, and is particularly delightful for strolling, as well as a fine spot to sit on hot days. (Contrary to popular belief, there are hot days here!) For the hardier, a visit on a heavily overcast or stormy winter's day can be rewarding too, as the imagination can get to work. Tynemouth Castle is one of the three castles within the boundaries of Tyne and Wear. The combination of priory, castle and grounds makes a visit a 'must'. The headland marks the northern side of the mouth of the Tyne.

Descending from the headland the visitor can walk 'out to sea' along the pier to the lighthouse, or take the upstream direction towards Collingwood's Monument. The monument is impressive, in keeping with the status of Collingwood, who was Nelson's second-in-command at Trafalgar and took over command when Nelson was killed. Four guns from Collingwood's ship *The Royal Sovereign*, on the four-square massive base of the monument, guard the entrance to the Tyne. Looking south from the monument the visitor will glimpse the first two beaches in a long sequence of beaches, shingly coves, rocky outcrops and stacks, which forms the eastern border of Tyne and Wear, south of the Tyne.

Almost all of the nearly 15-mile-long North Sea border of Tyne and Wear is walkable with great ease, by footpath, beach, grassland, and rocky cove.

As an alternative to the Metro from Tynemouth, the active visitor may like to walk along the riverside to the fish quay at North Shields. The fishing fleet which used to sail out proudly in line ahead bound for the Dogger Bank before the war is a shadow of its former self, but there is still a fair amount of activity at the quay. A ferry runs from North Shields to South Shields, a more interesting place largely because so much of old North Shields has been demolished. North Shields station once had an overall roof. This was demolished long ago and the present station although busy has no particular attraction.

Smith's Park, a new station, plagued by vandalism, comes next. Percy Main follows and just beyond can be seen the platform which is being built for a steam line planned to run to the Stephenson Museum at Middle Engine Lane, described on page 43. This line may well have a rosy future as there are proposals to extend it as a passenger line to Newbiggin and/or Ashington, which are both well beyond the boundaries of Tyne and Wear. There are major plans for development at the new closed-down Albert and Northumberland docks, including extending the steam railway southwards from Percy Main. It is sad indeed that the large complex network of railway lines which once served shipping has been taken away. Passengers for the ferries to Norway and Denmark are now bussed from Newcastle Central Station 8 miles away – a highly irritating procedure, especially for those who remember the days when they simply walked from the boat train, through the customs shed and straight on to the ship. Trains ran directly to the quay from places as far away as London.

After Howdon (the next station) the train crosses a viaduct over a valley which is itself worth a visit if time allows. The public open space is much more extensive than it appears from the viaduct. Hadrian Road and Wallsend are next. The names suggest much of Roman interest, but unfortunately although the remnants of Segedunum Fort at Wallsend have been laid out, they are nothing compared to Arbeia Fort in South Shields. The end of the wall was demolished to make way for a shipyard. Luckily somebody had the foresight to preserve the stones constituting the actual end of the wall, and they are at present in Richardson Dees Park. Permission has at last been given for them to be re-erected on the riverside walkway, planned to run most of the way from North Shields to Newcastle, using the track of the former Riverside BR electrified line.

After Wallsend the line continues westwards through an area of no special tourist merit. A giant hammerhead crane with a 'small' crane on top can still be seen in the distance. This small crane is actually quite big and best seen from the riverside walkway on the south side of the Tyne. Walkergate and Chillingham Road stations are

The lower Tyne near Wallsend (*Photo:* Harold Atkinson)

passed, and the yellow line reaches Byker through a cut-and-cover tunnel. Byker has become famous for the Byker Wall (no connection with Hadrian), the subject of often heated controversy. The Byker Wall is a long block of flats and maisonettes, so-called because the northern side has few windows (and those it does have are small) to protect the residents from the din and fumes of the dual-carriageway nearing completion alongside. The Wall is a few yards from the well-patronised Metro station.

After leaving Byker the visitor should look downwards. Beneath is the cutting which was once part of the electrified Riverside line. Part of the cutting is now filled in and the tunnel connecting it to the former BR electrified suburban system has been blocked off, thus ensuring that industry on the north bank of the Tyne will never again be served by railway. Beyond this cutting the yellow line crosses the architecturally quite famous Metro Bridge over the Ouseburn. To be appreciated this bridge has to be seen from below, from a small urban farm and adjacent parkland at the bottom of the valley. An ironwork railway bridge carrying the ECML and a road bridge complete the triplet of bridges over the Ouseburn. Downstream the burn is being developed with a marina, and the preservation of some old industrial buildings.

The line soon dives underground to Manors Metro station. Two platforms, now desolate and forlorn, are all that remain of the formerly very busy nine-platform Manors station. A somewhat rudimentary service of DMUs to Morpeth makes use of these platforms. Manors Metro station is new and designed for many more passengers than it has at present. Development in the vicinity will probably bring them. It is handy for the eastern side of Newcastle city centre except for one thing – the motorway which has to be crossed by a system of pedestrian-daunting bridges. The clock from the former Manors BR station now graces the Marsden Rattler pub and restaurant on South Shields sea-front. Use the green line to pay it a visit – you can eat in a railway carriage. The Marsden Rattler was a private line from South Shields to Whitburn colliery (long since defunct) but the public could use the trains available to workers at the colliery. Do not expect to see a colliery at Whitburn.

The yellow line tour is almost over. Monument is the next station and beyond it the terminus, St James, but not, we hope, for ever a terminus. The phenomenal success of the Metro system cries out for extension from St James to serve the large and, though they may not realise it, 'Metro-hungry' population west of the city centre. It is worth noticing that the station name is black on white – the colours of Newcastle United Football Club, whose ground, St James's Park, is a few yards away.

51

GREEN METRO LINE
by John Bourn

Bank Foot to South Shields

One thing railway lines do very well is to whisk you quickly from one environment into a totally different one. This Metro line demonstrates that very well, starting in the leafy, affluent suburbs of north-west Newcastle and finishing in the cheerful seaside atmosphere of South Shields. It is a line that is colour-coded green on the Metro map as well as being 'green' in environmental terms!

Kenton Bank Foot, on the rural fringes of Newcastle, is the current western terminus, but it is hoped that in 1991, trains will be running beyond the level-crossing at the end of the platform to Newcastle Airport, using the British Rail freight track currently *in situ* for most of its length. The Bill for construction of the extension has received royal assent and transport officials are now trying to secure EEC grants. Work was due to start in April 1990. The new line will also include a 'park and ride' station at Black Callerton, aimed at reducing road traffic into the city.

But for now, our journey starts at Bank Foot, on the only section of the Metro with a rural atmosphere, although even here, housing development for Newcastle's expanding commuter population threatens to swallow up the green fields. The first few stations, at Kingston Park, Fawdon, Wansbeck Road, and Regent Centre serve Newcastle suburbs, and are unlikely to be of great interest to the visitor. After Regent Centre, we pass the PTE's Metro workshops and sidings, and then join the coast loop line coming in on our left, as we arrive at South Gosforth, home of the Metro's computerised control centre.

We now run arrow-straight, bound for the heart of the city, passing the small halt at Ilford Road. The next station, West Jesmond, has been attractively converted from its BR days. Outside the station is an old-fashioned cinema, the Jesmond Picture House, the only cinema left in the Newcastle suburbs which has, thankfully, thus far survived competition from the slick but rather soulless 'multi-plexes'.

At the next station, Jesmond, the Metro plunges underground, moving through cast-iron or concrete tunnels bored into boulder clay or sandstone as far as Gateshead Stadium, where it returns to the surface. However we do abandon tunnel briefly in between to cross the River Tyne on the Queen Elizabeth II Bridge, opened by the H.M. The Queen in November 1981. Standing 81 feet above the water, the bridge's 540-foot-span is the largest over the river. Although most visitors to Newcastle will probably already have crossed the Tyne on one of the existing road or rail bridges, a crossing on a Metro train is still a memorable experience, as the train shoots out of its tunnel into the Tyne Gorge, high above the river, before plunging into tunnel once again.

Haymarket, Monument and Central Station Metro-stops all serve the city centre. Haymarket gives ready access to the Civic Centre, Newcastle Playhouse and the northern tip of the Eldon Square Shopping Centre; Monument is closer to the main section of Eldon Square, the Recreation Centre, Theatre Royal, Odeon Cinema, and the main shopping streets. Central Station gives direct access to BR services, is close to the Tyne Theatre and Newcastle Arts Centre, the Quayside, and of course the castle. Keen photographers will want to climb the winding steps to the battlements for a magnificent view of the city and the river; and railway buffs will appreciate the panoramic view of the eastern end of the station. (A more detailed description of the city appears on page 58.)

The next station, Gateshead, is ideally-situated for the town centre, with ample car-parking, and a shopping precinct opposite the Metro station. From here you can also visit Saltwell Park, the North East's largest. There is a boating lake, rides for children, animals on display, a wooded dene and numerous secluded spots even on the busiest of summer days. Take a packed lunch as catering is limited. To get there, catch the 53 or 54 bus from the bottom stand at Gateshead's Metro Interchange (i.e., the one furthest away from the station exit). The buses run every few minutes and the journey time is about ten minutes on the 53, slightly longer on the 54.

Gateshead's art gallery, leisure centre and library (housing the Tourist Information Centre) are near the park, as are most of the town's hotels and boarding houses.

Back on the Metro train, we now reach Gateshead Stadium station, although the stadium is a good ten minutes' walk away. Famous for its athletics events, the stadium is also the home of HFS Loans League side, Gateshead F.C.

The stadium can be seen in the distance on the left-hand side of the train, as we approach our next stop, Felling. After this comes Heworth, interchange station with many local bus services and BR trains to Sunderland. Pelaw comes next, followed by carriage sidings for trains terminating at Pelaw. We cross the Sunderland line on a flyover and then run single-track for a while, although Metro authorities hope to convert this section to double-track. The adjacent track is used by BR freight trains.

We are now entering South Tyneside, a borough being aggressively marketed to tourists as 'Catherine Cookson Country'; an example of tourist chiefs turning a region's literary associations (things have changed a lot from the world described in Catherine Cookson's books, but the old image of pit heaps and grime still lingers in the minds of those outside the region!) to its own advantage.

There are views of the Tyne on our left, although now very different from the sylvan views you can enjoy on British Rail's Tyne Valley Line; it is now an old, tired, grimy river, although the industry along the riverbanks, particularly shipbuilding, is not what it was. Where there is dereliction, there is usually graffiti: it is prominent on factory walls lining the route, drawn by self-proclaimed 'Arts Masters'.

Hebburn station comes next, then Jarrow, famous for its 1936 Hunger March, commemorated by a mural on the station platform, which was unveiled by Neil Kinnock. Jarrow also has religious associations: the Venerable Bede worshipped in St Paul's church here 1,300 years ago. The church is five minutes' walk from our next stop, named (what else?) Bede.

We call at Tyne Dock station, then the underground station at Chichester (pronounced 'Chy-chester'). We run over a bridge, with South Shields up ahead, and then into South Shields station, overlooking the shopping centre. Although the main station is newly-built, the former BR station is still in use as an alternative exit at the far end of the platform. However, this is now planned for demolition.

South Shields
The main exit from the Metro station is on King Street, at the heart of South Shields' shopping centre. Turn left and you come to the market place, rebuilt following extensive bomb damage in World War II. The market square is dominated by the Old Town Hall, built in 1768, the only building in the square to survive a 1941 bombing raid. Continue ahead through the market square, bearing slightly right, and you will come to the ferry terminal from which there is a frequent service across the river into North Shields, where you can link up with the Metro again.

The town centre is linked to the sea-front by Ocean Road, about half a mile in length, with a variety of seaside boarding houses down the left-hand side, and on the right, a mixture of amusement emporia, cafés, and fast-food takeaways, of variable quality. At the sea-front, there is a fairground and two parks. North Marine Park climbs up onto the cliffs overlooking the sea and the river estuary, and offers fine views and breezy, brisk walking. South Marine Park will probably have more attractions for children, with a boating lake and miniature steam railway running around the lake.

Arbeia Fort reconstructed gateway at South Shields (*Photo:* Harold Atkinson)

Marsden Rattler pub and restaurant at South Shields (*Photo:* Harold Atkinson)

There is also a Roman fort in South Shields, known as Arbeia, sign-posted from the town centre (it is actually situated on Baring Street, north of Ocean Road). Built in about AD 128, the fort, in the process of being completely excavated, served as a Roman supply base and guarded the entrance to the Tyne, enabling supplies to be brought up from further south.

After early growth as a holiday resort, fuelled by the arrival of the railway, South Shields has not found things easy in recent years. During the 1980s however, the local councils have, with some success, devoted a lot of time and effort to tidying up the town and shaking off the somewhat run-down air it had acquired. Although it could do with a wider variety of eating places, it makes a pleasant destination for a day out.

There are good bus links from Shields to Marsden and Whitburn, the latter a particularly attractive village with a thirteenth-century church. At Marsden, the famous Marsden Rock, once joined to the mainland, but not standing 100 yards offshore, is colonised by numerous sea-birds, making it the North East's second most important bird colony. The nearby Marsden Grotto, now a pub-cum-café, is a fascinating affair, originally built in the 1780s by a miner known as Jack the Blaster, who cut out a home for his family among the caves in the limestone cliffs. A clifftop path links Marsden and Whitburn. Just south of the latter is Seaburn, a minor seaside resort and suburb of Sunderland, with a station on the BR route to Newcastle.

DARLINGTON
by Marc Lewis

It has to be said that the rail approaches to Darlington from either north or south are scarcely likely to tempt the traveller to stop and explore the south-west corner of County Durham. Indeed, the vista of derelict factories and demolition sites may make one think that the 1197 Exchequer valuation of the Borough at £8 is still about right!

First impressions are, however, often deceptive and visitors expecting to find a typical northern industrial town will be surprised at County Durham's largest urban area. Darlington's population of some 97,000 people is large enough to support excellent commercial, cultural, sporting and transport facilities, but still small enough to be relaxed and friendly.

Passengers arriving on InterCity or local TeesRail trains will normally use Bank Top station, which is on a loop just off the East Coast Main Line. Most trains call at the station's very wide island platform, although freight services and a few InterCity trains run past on the main line.

In the 1980s, British Rail refurbished the station and repaired its fine overall roof. At the end of the bay platforms 2 and 3, at the south end, can be seen a display of maps and pictures commemorating the Stockton & Darlington Railway, although Bank Top was the creation of the Great North of England Railway in 1841. The Stockton & Darlington had a branch from their station at North Road, 1¼ miles to the north-west, down along the course of the present main line and then slightly to the west of it as far as Croft Spa on the River Tees, but this was used for goods only.

Bank Top, referred to in present-day timetables simply as Darlington, has all the facilities of an InterCity station, including buffet and travel centre.

On leaving the station by the ramp at the northern end, one can take a blue and cream Darlington Transport bus, or white United minibus, to the town centre at High Row.

The short journey into town passes the Civic Theatre, which offers an impressive selection of plays each season, St Cuthbert's church, and the Town Museum where the industrial, social and natural history of the area is interpreted.

Darlington's heart is the High Row and Market Place, with attractive Victorian clock tower and market hall. It was mercifully saved from re-development into a concrete shopping centre in the early 1970s. Behind the market hall can be found a number of public houses and restaurants. For the sports-minded, the Dolphin Centre offers excellent facilities at moderate cost, and for those who prefer just to watch others working up a sweat, a small admission fee gives access to the bar and restaurant as well.

Opposite the Dolphin Centre are the modern headquarters of the Borough Council and St Cuthbert's church, which is believed to date from the establishment of the town in Saxon times. Certainly the known history of the building dates from 1084 and work started on the present structure in 1180. St Cuthbert's is a fine example of medieval ecclesiastical architecture and is often referred to as the 'Lady of the North'.

Further down Feethams from the church is the United Automobile bus station. After St Cuthbert's this is less than an architectural triumph, but is a good place to start an excursion to the attractive, and once rail-served, dale market towns of Richmond in North Yorkshire and Barnard Castle in County Durham's Teesdale.

To the west of the bus station is Houndgate, where the family home of Joseph Pease, prominent local Quaker, banker and promoter of the Stockton & Darlington Railway, is still in use as an office. On the far western side of the town centre, opposite Stanhope Green, is the Arts Centre where exhibitions, concerts, plays and other cultural activities can be enjoyed. The building itself was originally a teachers' training college, the style of which could be termed 'municipal gothic'.

Darlington offers the usual range of chain stores as well as a great variety of smaller, more personal establishments. Visitors with an eye for a bargain will be unable to resist the large open-air market held on Mondays and Saturdays, which attracts crowds of people from the surrounding rural areas. Early-closing day is Wednesday.

Entrance to Durham Castle (*Photo:* Harold Atkinson)

CITY OF DURHAM
by Geoffrey Roper

Described as 'one of the great experiences of Europe' by Sir Nikolaus Pevsner, the city of Durham is a very special, indeed unique place, to which no discerning visitor to the region can fail to make a pilgrimage. Its magnificence can hardly be seen to better advantage than from the railway station, situated on high land to the west of the town, from which the arriving visitor can see straight across to the great fortified rock on which stand the splendid and almost overpowering ensemble of cathedral, monastery and castle.

The cathedral, built around the shrine of St Cuthbert and dating in its earliest parts to the 1090s, is one of the most important romanesque (Norman) buildings in Europe, and almost certainly the first to feature rib-vaulting, on which the later development of Gothic architecture wholly depended. Its 'consummate mastery of scale and proportion' (to quote Pevsner again) makes it unforgettable in itself; its stupendous setting adds to the overwhelming awe which any sensitive visitor must feel.

The monastic buildings to the south of the cathedral are unusual in having largely escaped the ruin which most others suffered after the Dissolution, and can be seen for the most part in their original state. The Monks' Dormitory and Treasury museums should not be missed, and the undercroft restaurant has well revived the monastic traditions of good food and drink. Beyond these lies College Green (the cathedral close), a peaceful and beautiful haven.

The castle is also Norman (started 1072), and was the residence of the Prince-Bishops of the Palatinate of Durham until 1837, when it passed to the university: it then became, and still is, University College. Its ancient structure is well preserved: especially worth seeing are the numinous Norman chapel, the sumptuous twelfth-century doorway of Bishop le Puiset, the Great Hall and the magnificent seventeenth-century Black Staircase. (Access by conducted tour only.)

Between the castle and the cathedral lies Palace Green, a large open space surrounded by university buildings. East of them run North and South Bailey, medieval streets which, as their names indicate, are within the fortified area commonly called the Peninsula. This is formed by a very sharp bend, almost a loop, in the River Wear between the medieval Framwellgate and Elvet bridges. The street layout of the town is consequently rather confusing to the newcomer, to whom it sometimes seems that there are two rivers. Maps and leaflets can, however, be obtained from the Tourist Information Office in the Market Place, along with other useful information, such as lists of hotels and guest houses.

A stroll around the town should take in the several ancient churches, one of which, St Mary-le-Bow by the east end of the cathedral, is now a 'Heritage Centre'; and the beautiful wooded river banks, which afford memorable glimpses of the old town high above them. South Street, accessible from the foot of Crossgate, has many attractive old houses, and also provides a splendid view of the west end of the cathedral across the river. A visit should also be paid to the Elvet district to the east, which contains the medieval St Oswald's church, the famous Gaol and court-house, and several fine Georgian terraces. Beyond lies the old racecourse, which every July is the focus of the annual Durham Miners' Gala, at once an industrial, political and recreational occasion. Many of the miners and their families used to arrive at the old Elvet station alongside; it was, alas, demolished in 1964, but part of the original embankment and bridge abutments may still be seen. Another, much older station building still survives, however, over the river in Gilesgate. Built in 1844, in an elegant classical style, it was Durham's first station, then at the end of a branch line, and is now a hardware store.

As well as occupying many of the town's old buildings, the university has in recent years been an important patron of modern architecture. Especially notable is its Dunelm House, nestling on the river bank, below the soaring Kingsgate footbridge. Many of the new college and university buildings are out to the south of the town, where the Oriental Museum can also be found, with its important collection of Asiatic works of art and Egyptian antiquities. Other museums are the Archaeological Museum in the old Fulling Mill on the riverbank below the cathedral, and the Durham Light Infantry Museum at Aykley Heads, which also houses an art gallery.

Further afield, the area around Durham abounds with delightful wooded country-side. Especially enjoyable are the walks through Kepier Woods, past the fourteenth-century Kepier Hospital; Pelaw Woods (below Gilesgate); and along the banks of the River Browney beyond Neville's Cross. The ruins of Finchale Priory, a monastic rest-house exquisitely situated by the wooded riverbanks 3½ miles to the north-east, are also well worth visiting.

Before boarding the train, the departing visitor should allow time to ascend to Wharton Park, just above the station to the west, where from the mock battlements a final sweeping view can be had over the whole city, with the station and the massive eleven-arch viaduct of 1857, which carries the line away to the south.

NEWCASTLE-UPON-TYNE
by Harold Atkinson

New Castle! The name seems to betoken the city's origin. Does it? No. It marks a momentous turning-point in its history and a resurrection from obscurity. The turning-point was so momentous that the date, 1080, is celebrated as the birthday of Newcastle. The city's real origins are hazy indeed. The earliest recorded name, Pons Aelii, is Roman. Pons Aelii preceded the building of the Roman Wall which was begun in AD 122. After the departure of the Romans, the town (for it was not yet a city) drifted back into obscurity. For much of the time it was called Monkchester and was adjacent to Pandon. The Roman name, 'Bridge of Aelius', draws attention to one of the city's features; bridges, not all of them over the river. Some of the bridges, over valleys long since filled in, remain in name only as, for example, High Bridge, Barras Bridge.

This short introduction cannot be, nor is it intended to be, a substitute for the pamphlets, brochures, and booklets available at the information centre in the Central Library. This library is in Princess Square close to the lower (south) end of Northumberland Street, a very short walk from Monument Metro station. The visitor is recommended to study the literature over a cup of coffee or tea in the library and plan a preliminary exploratory walk.

A suggested preliminary exploratory walk with the Town Walls as a connecting thread
As Newcastle and the whole country, indeed the whole world, owe so much to railways, and as the North East in the 'cradle' of railways, it is fitting to start an exploration at Central Station. Grainger Street leads directly to Earl Gray's Monument from Central Station, and is one of the principal streets in the carefully planned area dating from about 1830 and completed in Victorian times. At that time the centre of activity of Newcastle was shifting up from the riverside. After exploring this area (on another day) the visitor must decide for him- or herself whether the writer is guilty of over-statement when he asserts that Newcastle can compete on equal terms architecturally with Bath.

Using the plan on the back of the pamphlet 'Blackfriars' the visitor should make his/her way to Bath Lane where there is a relatively long stretch of wall, with gardens on the outer side. The tower here is the Durham Tower. At the end of this part of the wall turn right into Stowell Street and go down to Blackfriars, a recently-restored monastery dating from about the thirteenth century. Blackfriars has an above-average buffet, and serves tea and coffee in real cups and saucers. The menu is well varied and includes lunches. Until 1989 there was a good information centre within its walls, with a character which the library centre does not have. It is to be hoped that pressure to reinstate it succeeds.

The visitor should retrace his/her steps to Bath Lane, turn right, and almost immediately right again onto a grassed area from which there is a good view of the outer side of the longest stretch of surviving wall in Newcastle. On the inner side of the wall is a narrow cobbled alleyway giving an atmosphere of antiquity but it needs a good clean up. This alleyway is the back of Stowell Street, which is becoming a Chinese Quarter and which will, if plans go right, soon have a Chinese Arch. Stowell Street will appeal to lovers of Chinese food but not to the architecturally sensitive.

Next on the route is St Andrew's church. It is at the Newgate Street end of Darn Crook, now renamed St Andrew's Street, and can be located easily by using the map on the back of the 'Blackfriars' pamphlet. St Andrew's is reputed to be the oldest church in Newcastle (but not in Tyne and Wear). It has another claim to fame: within its churchyard is a stretch of wall which forms part of the structure of a listed building. Hence only one side can be seen. Perhaps one day the owners of the building will provide access for visitors to view the other side.

A useful route (there are several possibilities) now is to go down Newgate Street and turn right, along Clayton Street. At present Clayton Street is somewhat shabby, but architecturally good. It becomes West Clayton Street beyond its intersection with Westgate Road. This part of Clayton Street has been done up and shows what the other part could, and should, look like. Go down Bewick Street to the Central Station and follow the station frontage, past the Royal Station Hotel, and turn right through the tunnel to Orchard Street. In Orchard Street there is a rather good stretch of wall, about a hundred yards long and standing virtually full height. It was revealed to public gaze several years ago when the Federation Brewery was demolished. The Council missed an excellent opportunity to boost the tourist appeal of Newcastle when it failed to lay out the surrounding ground as gardens to display this part of the

Part of the High Level Bridge which the walkway passes under at high level (*Photo: Harold Atkinson*)

St Nicholas's Cathedral, Newcastle
(*Photo:* Harold Atkinson)

wall to maximum effect. Instead it permitted a large car park on one side, a car park and a building supplier's yard on the other.

On the end of this piece of wall is a plaque with an intriguing reference to 'Breakneck Steps'. The visitor cannot put the aptness of the name to the test as the steps no longer exist, and so should walk to the bank-top and peer down at the recently-exposed foundations of the part of the wall which ran down to the river. Breakneck Steps were approximately alongside. The visitor will be satisfied that the name was well-earned. Without descending to the riverside the visitor should explore the foot-paths in a downstream direction until the path system ends and an old stone archway is seen on the left. This archway leads to the castle. Following the path from near Breakneck Steps area to the end near the castle however can be tricky. At what seems to be a deadend, turn left *up* the stone steps and then first right (before the top of the steps). The visitor is not near the end of the path system until after passing *under* (at about mid-level) the approach arches of the High Level Bridge (an easily-recognisable double-decker bridge).

On taking the route behind the castle and through the Black Gate, St Nicholas's Cathedral will be seen (not built as a cathedral but designated as such when Newcastle became a city). The Lantern Tower of St Nicholas's is possibly Newcastle's crowning glory. It is said to be the finest of its type in existence, and this is not difficult to believe. This tower seems to compete with the New Tyne Bridge (the arched bridge) as unofficial symbol of Newcastle, much as St Paul's often symbolises London. The cathedral and castle should be noted for a visit on another day.

The visitor should go back to and through the old archway and down the steps to the Quayside. There are several other examples of steep steps, characteristic of medieval Newcastle. Turn left at the bottom, past some sixteenth-century houses, and turn right at the end to pass under the New Tyne Bridge (not really new – opened in 1928). This riverside area is where Newcastle began. Most of the buildings now are Victorian and of architectural merit, worth looking at, especially when cleaned up (as some have been). This part of Newcastle had the most concentrated area of 'chares'. Chares are medieval, often extremely narrow, alleyways. Many survived until the late 1940s and early 1950s but most now exist merely as names on walls.

The visitor should go up King Street and climb the steps to All Saints church. Circular churches are not exceptionally rare but elliptical ones like this are. On looking eastwards from the churchyard, the Sallyport Tower can be seen. The Corner Tower is seen on looking northwards and, also, leading steeply downwards from it, a portion of the wall which lost the fight when City Road was built. If the visitor threads his/her way through All Saints Office Precinct he/she will arrive at The Holy Jesus Hospital (now the Joicey Museum). It is worth visiting at leisure another day. The museum incorporates the Austin Tower which was revealed during demolition work about twenty years ago.

A suggested choice for ending the walk is via the labyrinth of paths and subways of the Pilgrim Street roundabout, to Moseley Street. Swan House, the North East head-quarters of British Telecom, occupies the centre of the roundabout. In it can be seen a replica of part of the interior of the Royal Arcade, which was demolished to make way for the roundabout. The visitor should buy a postcard of the Royal Arcade at the Information centre to see what Newcastle sacrificed in order to gain a roundabout. The visitor should go westwards to the bottom of the dip in Moseley Street and there turn right into Grey Street with its curve of gracious façades, which will take him/her to the Monument.

This sample walk could be enjoyed in the course of a day or in part another day at a leisurely pace.

Newcastle is not at the top of the list for tourism in England. Nevertheless the visitor is virtually certain to go away thinking that it has been time very well spent.

BERWICK-UPON-TWEED

by Alister Blades

This station stands on the site of the great hall of Berwick Castle. Here in 17.11.1292 the claim of Robert Bruce to the crown of Scotland was declined and the decision in favour of John Balliol was given by King Edward I before the full Parliament of England and a large gathering of the nobility and populace of both England and Scotland.

This notice at the foot of Berwick station footbridge prepares you for the historic significance of this most northerly of English towns. It is now a bustling community of 12,000 people, but it had a particularly turbulent history before the Union of England and Scotland in 1603, as its fortifications still testify.

At the end of the station approach road, turn right, following the main street, Marygate, as far as the arch of the Scotsgate. The Tourist Information Office, close by, is open from April to October. From the gate, there is a good view down the wide shopping street to the imposing eighteenth-century Town Hall which includes the former jail, now a museum.

To the right, you can follow the town ramparts to Megs Mount, a bastion which gives splendid views of the Tweed with its two road bridges, the older of which dates from the seventeenth century, and the remains of the medieval walls.

Returning to Scotsgate, the visitor is recommended to follow the Elizabethan ramparts round towards the sea, noting the seventeenth-century cannon on Cumberland Bastion and the fine coastal view from Brass Bastion.

Crossing over the Cowport, the only gateway surviving in its original form, we pass the Parish Church and Barracks on the right. The Barracks are the earliest built in Britain and now contain a museum of military history, open throughout the year.

Two more bastions are passed and the garrison Magazine (also open to the public), before we proceed down Kipper Hill (with its former smokehouses) to Fisher's Fort with its Crimean War cannon and a pier and small sandy beach nearby.

This quiet part of the town also contains the Lindisfarne Wine and Spirit Museum and the house of the former Military Governor. A walk back along the Quay Walls to the Old Bridge gives the chance to view an attractive variety of architectural styles before turning right and back into the busy shopping area of Marygate.

The bus station, in this street, has services to Holy Island (service 477) twice a day, and Bamburgh (no. 466) three times a day. Service 463 runs five times a day inland via Norham (where the old station is now a museum) to Coldstream, with connections or through-workings to Kelso. Service 360 to Galashiels via Duns and Melrose is of similar frequency while about a dozen buses a day (services 473 and 464) run from Berwick to Wooler.

FURTHER INFORMATION

Northumbria Tourist Board, Aykley Heads, Durham, publishes an annual guide which gives details of all places of interest and selected accommodation. This guide is obtainable from the Board (as are a number of more detailed local guides), from more than thirty Tourist Information Offices and from many bookshops.

MAPS A good map is essential for the country walks suggested in this book, and is desirable for cycle rides. Ordnance Survey publish maps of various scales, each series suited for particular purposes. For details, write to Information and Public Enquiries, Ordnance Survey, Romsey Road, Maybush, Southampton SO9 4DH. Other useful maps are in the National series published by John Bartholomew & Sons, Duncan Street, Edinburgh EH9 1TA.

TIMETABLES British Rail publish a Passenger Timetable of over 1,600 pages for the whole country. This is issued in May and October each year, sometimes with supplements, and can be bought at staffed stations and booksellers. Free timetable booklets and leaflets are also available for individual lines or groups of lines at staffed stations, as are leaflets on the carriage of bicycles by train. It should be noted that carriage of bicycles on Pacer trains is limited, but free. A small charge is usually made, and prior reservation advisable, on Sprinter and InterCity 125 trains.

BUS INFORMATION Bus deregulation introduced under the 1986 Transport Act means that information about services can quickly become out-of-date. We cannot accept any responsibility for such information, but we can recommend the publications of at least two County Councils in the North East:

Durham County Council, Transport Information Section, Environment Department, County Hall, Durham DH1 5UQ (tel. 091-386 4411 x 2337), publish a very handy *Tourist Travel Guide*, free of charge. This pocket-sized booklet lists all important towns and villages, with market days, transport operators, journey times, fares and departure times.

A series of *Town Travel Guides* is also published, containing full bus and train timetables for the relevant locality. 50p postage is requested for these.

Three countryside leaflet packs give descriptions of some twenty interesting walks.

Many of these publications are also available at information centres, libraries and newsagents. Finally, a *County Travel Guide Ring Binder* can also be bought from the County Council.

Northumberland County Council, Public Transport Team, County Hall, Morpeth, Northumberland, NE61 2EF (tel. 0670 514343), publish a comprehensive *Public Transport Guide* at £1.00 (plus 50p postage) in a winter and summer edition. The summer edition includes an expanded tourist information section with details of places to visit, how to get there by public transport and a 'What's on in Northumberland' feature. This very useful book also has the addresses and telephone numbers of libraries, bus operators, hospitals, and even a summary of shipping and air services.

The guide can be bought or consulted at bus inquiry offices, libraries and tourist information offices. Also available is an attractive public transport route-map with town centre plans.

Doe's Bus/Rail Guide is another very handy publication which gives information about services between railheads and principal non-rail-served destinations, including most places of over 7,000 population and many smaller tourist centres. It is obtainable at £4.50 (post free) from B.S. Doe, 25 Newmorton Road, Moordown, Bournemouth, Dorset BH9 3NU. The guide is issued once a quarter, and you can also take out an annual subscription at £15.00.

Also available from the same address is *Doe's Directory of Bus Timetables* which lists bus operators on a county-by-county basis and costs £2.50.

COME AND JOIN US!

The **Railway Development Society** is a voluntary, national, independent body which campaigns for better rail services for both passengers and freight, and greater use of rail transport.

It publishes books and reports, holds meetings and exhibitions, sometimes runs special trains, and puts the rail users' point of view to politicians, commerce and industry, local government officials and civil servants, as well as referring users' comments and suggestions to British Rail management and unions.

There are fifteen branches of the Society, covering all of Great Britain. The North East Branch covers the counties of Northumberland, Tyne and Wear, Co. Durham and Cleveland. Its Secretary is Geoffrey Longstaff, 3 Newton Street, Witton Gilbert, Co. Durham DH7 6SN.

Membership is open to all who are in general agreement with the aims of the Society, and subscriptions (as at March 1990) are:

Standard rate: **£7.50**

Pensioners, students and unemployed: **£4.00**

Families: **£7.50** plus £1.00 for each member of household

The Membership Secretary is Mr. F. J. Hastilow, 49 Irnham Road, Sutton Coldfield, West Midlands B74 2TQ.

For further information about the Society, write to the General Secretary, Trevor Garrod, 15 Clapham Road, Lowestoft, Suffolk NR32 1RQ.

Transport 2000, the national federation of organisations campaigning for better public transport and protection of the environment, has two local branches. These are:

Northumbria: Don Kent, 12 Brunel Street, Ferryhill, Co. Durham.

Cleveland: Peter Walker, 26 Devon Crescent, Billingham, Cleveland.

Lindisfarne Castle, Holy Island
(*Photo:* Northumbria Tourist Board)

ISBN: 0–7117–0529–1
© Railway Development Society 1990
Published by Jarrold Publishing, Norwich
Printed in Great Britain. 2/90